DETROIT

DETROIT
THREE PATHWAYS TO REVITALIZATION

LEWIS D. SOLOMON

Transaction Publishers
New Brunswick (U.S.A.) and London (U.K.)

Library of Congress Catalog Number: 2013005195
ISBN: 978-1-4128-5196-1
Printed in the United States of America

Library of Congress Cataloging-in-Publication Data

Solomon, Lewis D.
  Detroit : three pathways to revitalization / Lewis D. Solomon.
      pages cm
  ISBN 978-1-4128-5196-1 (alk. paper)
  1. Detroit (Mich.)--Economic conditions. 2. Detroit (Mich.)--Social conditions. 3. Public schools--Michigan--Detroit. I. Title.
  HC108.D6S65 2013
  338.9774'34--dc23
                                                        2013005195

In memory of
Irving Louis Horowitz

Contents

Introduction

As America's most dysfunctional big city, Detroit currently faces many challenges characteristic of advanced urban decay, including massive population losses; fractured neighborhoods with many impoverished households; an uneducated, unskilled workforce; too few jobs; a shrinking tax base; budgetary shortfalls; and inadequate public schools. Thus, Detroit represents a symbol of urban poverty that must deal with its demographic, economic, and spatial realities and the accompanying political, legal, and even psychological hurdles. As one expert gloomily concluded:

> Many shrinking cities seem unable to overcome the forces causing depopulation. Nor are they able to deflect the burdens faced by their governments, households, and businesses. Opportunities are scarcer than in growing cities; metropolitan economies are not as robust, job growth is relatively anemic and fewer jobs are available, and less wealth is being generated. Immigrants who might occupy homes and open businesses are less likely to locate in shrinking cities. [W]hile these cities are more likely to have higher percentages of African-Americans. As a result, fewer people work in shrinking cities and household incomes are lower. These factors burden the local housing market, as well. Home values barely appreciate, chronic vacancy is prevalent, and an older housing stock is neither upgraded nor replaced. Here, housing is not a source of wealth. Moreover, the local governments can hardly be of much assistance, constrained as they are by diminishing tax bases and expanding demands to demolish abandoned housing, replace aged infrastructure, and offer services for an increasingly dependent population.
>
> In sum, the depopulation of metropolitan areas, cities, suburbs, and neighborhoods poses significant challenges for policy makers at the local, state, and federal levels. For local government officials in these cities, shrinkage and its consequences are unavoidable and civic leaders struggle with how to respond. The pursuit of growth and past glory seems ill-advised. "Rightsizing" makes sense, but how to do it is neither obvious nor politically palatable. Therein lies the challenge.[1]

Faced with a multiplicity of challenges, Detroit and its residents must realistically accept the current conditions and the difficult, short-term public sector fiscal remedies. Detroiters must also assess the possibility of an achievable future over the intermediate and long term, taking advantage of the city's assets and rebuilding a political economy around them as well as new businesses and new types of organizations. However, even acknowledging the city's shrinkage and the multitude of obstacles to revitalization represents a political risk to present and future mayors, council members, and civic leaders.

Looking to the future, this book focuses on three pathways to revitalizing Detroit, offering a cautiously optimistic view set in the realistic context of a shrinking municipality marked by massive losses of people and jobs, and other problems, such as the longstanding racial divide between the city and its suburbs. Tackling the challenges one by one, it urges a viable economic development strategy anchored in Detroit balancing its municipal and public school district's budgets, improving the academic performance of its public schools, rebuilding its tax base, and looking to the for-profit private sector to create jobs for its residents, thereby enabling them to pursue their own economic future.

This book advocates an overlapping, tripartite political economy. It builds on the foundation of a rightsized public sector and a resurgent for-profit private sector with the latter fueling economic growth. Although facing a long, tough road to implementation, it sketches a vision of an alternative economic sector based on the constructive use of two key assets: vacant land and unskilled labor lacking high levels of formal education or training. In this new political economy, the public sector and the private sector—consisting of nonprofit organizations, foundations, and established business firms and start-ups, together with new community-oriented entities, such as cooperatives—would coexist and function alongside each other. In other words, Detroit could build a local, more sustainable political economy in addition to, not in replacement of, the web of big government and big corporations currently set in the context of the global financial system.

This book consists of four parts. The first part provides background and context on Detroit. It offers a brief overview of the city's numerous challenges in chapter 1. These negatives include precipitous population losses, a shrinking tax base, too few jobs, an uneducated, unskilled workforce, and fractured neighborhoods with many impoverished families. Human capital and labor-market challenges exist. Divisiveness and distrust abound and hold back renewal.[2] It is uncertain whether the legacy of distrust among city hall, business and foundation interests, and community residents can be overcome. The totality of these liabilities poses significant obstacles, at least in the short and intermediate term, to Detroit's revitalization.

Chapter 2 summarizes Detroit's assets. It focuses on numerous anchor institutions, including for-profit businesses and nonprofit organizations, such as universities, health care centers, and locally and nationally based foundations.

The second part begins by examining Detroit's immediate efforts to overcome its fiscal crisis in chapter 3, with the appointment of an emergency manager in March 2013, seemingly averting insolvency and putting the city on the path to financial stability and sustainability. The odds of success in this endeavor appear high, despite the opposition of public sector unions and their political allies. However, the specter of bankruptcy looms over Detroit, particularly if the city cannot bring its falling revenues in line with its expenses.

Chapter 4 analyzes the city's need in the intermediate term (three to five years) to rightsize its public sector and provide quality public services. The city must not only continue to balance its budget and eliminate its accumulated deficit; it must also continue to provide essential services, such as public safety, over its sprawling area.

Scarce public financial resources may lead to innovation. Detroit must try to shore up its stable neighborhoods and retain middle-class taxpayers. Mayor Dave Bing's attempt to reshape the delivery of municipal services petered out. A 2011 short-term action plan, implemented in three demonstration areas, achieved only modest, if not tepid, results. Rationalizing public services beyond these efforts will likely prove difficult. The 2012 long-term plan, the Detroit Strategic Framework Plan, a visionary document, will probably sit on the shelf, with low odds for comprehensive implementation, at least for the foreseeable future. The plan suffers, furthermore, from a notable deficiency: the lack of any type of funding mechanism. However, the Kresge Foundation pledged $100 million over the next five years to assist in implementing the plan.

In addition to putting its school district on a sound financial footing, Detroit must also provide residents' children with a knowledge base for future success by improving the academic performance of its K–12 public schools, as discussed in chapter 5. As a result of the efforts of an emergency financial manager and an emergency manager, the Detroit Public School District appears on its way to achieving financial viability. It appears probable that the system will continue on the path to fiscal sustainability, particularly with the enactment of the 2012 Local Financial Stability and Choice Act. Hopefully the district will keep expenses in line with revenues and continue to generate budgetary surpluses despite falling enrollments.

Student academic gains and increased high school graduation rates represent more difficult tasks, particularly in view of some parents' seeming disinterest in their children's education and a lack of character training in some homes and in the public schools. With the 2012 legislation, effective in March 2013, those resistant to change—the teachers' union and their school board allies—will not control decision making with respect to academics.

These are all difficult endeavors as critically analyzed in chapters 3, 4, and 5. However, the first stirrings of progress occurred beginning in 2009 after decades of free fall.

The third part of this book considers how Detroit can implement a new approach to job creation, one focused on the for-profit private sector, not the public sector. A resurgent, more diversified for-profit private sector, in the intermediate and long term, will help propel the city's economic growth and provide sustained employment opportunities. As jobs and incomes grow, so will Detroit's tax revenues. As considered in chapter 6, corporate relocations into the city and financial repopulation incentives will facilitate economic development. Although rebuilding Detroit's tax base and aiding its retail sector, the transfer of workers will not significantly reduce Detroit's unemployment rate. Most firms shifted existing workers from the suburbs to the city. Even with financial repopulation incentives, it is unclear whether downtown and certain key areas, such as Midtown, will develop sufficient density. Whole Foods's decision to open a store in Midtown, however, points to one savvy company's bet on the vitality of a new urban core in Detroit.

It is a challenge for Detroit and its residents in the twenty-first century to use scarce traditional public and private resources to achieve the maximum impact. In an era of public sector fiscal austerity, a need exists for a collaborative strategy among existing institutions: all levels of government; the for-profit private sector; and nonprofit entities, such as foundations. As part of a collaborative approach, Detroit will likely witness the implementation of more public-private partnerships. However, the most notable public-private partnership, the M-1 Light Rail project, failed to come to fruition.

The economic development and employment gains generated by entrepreneurs, who build companies and employ people, will help revitalize the city. As analyzed in chapters 6 and 7, skepticism exists, however, as to the ability of the for-profit private sector to create the massive numbers of needed, new jobs. The widely heralded Creative Class will likely play a more limited role in job creation than entrepreneurs, more generally. The gap between the white "creatives" and the black residents will probably perpetuate the city's racial divide.

Detroit's human-capital challenge, as discussed in chapter 7, presents a significant barrier to economic development and job creation. A mismatch exists between available jobs, now and likely in the future, and residents' skills and education. Although workforce development efforts require more funding, the track record of past and current job-training endeavors generally offers only a slight possibility of success. Moreover, it remains difficult to overcome job sprawl in Detroit, that is, the imbalance between where people live and jobs are located. The creation of a regional transit authority offers hope in overcoming the spatial mismatch.

In the book's fourth part, as developed in chapter 8, during the intermediate and long term, residents could pursue a bottom-up strategy[3] based on the actions of individuals and community groups rather than looking to large-scale projects—such as auto assembly plants or the redevelopment of downtown through casinos and sports stadiums. Although facing long odds of implementation, Detroiters could build an alternative political economy sector based on community gardens, cooperative businesses, and a local currency. The public sector could assist this development by allowing its land-use policies to enhance the viability of agriculture in the city. Integrating a broad range of food-system elements—production, processing, and distribution—into an urban development strategy would further enhance this approach. Building on a community-based food system could enable Detroit and its residents to help achieve broader goals, such as labor-intensive employment and sustainable economic vitality as an alternative to the prevailing consumer lifestyle.[4] In this parallel economy, people could obtain their basic needs—food, shelter, clothing, education, and health care. A community-based sector, characterized by a higher degree of local self-reliance, might see a reduction in our consumer-driven culture—marked by mindless economic growth and unsustainable consumerism, characterized by the acquisition of designer-label clothing and accessories as well as the latest electronic devices.

The development of community-based entities from within rests, however, on involving people in building an emerging, parallel political economy sector based on the foundation of residents', associations', and institutions' assets, skills, and capabilities. Uncertainty, if not skepticism, exists, however, whether it will be possible to spark this type of self-initiated, grassroots revival—a rebirth designed to empower residents, enabling each to achieve his or her potential, not merely allowing them to exist ever more dependently on the public sector in the current welfare system.

Although the alternative political economy sector represents a rational approach to Detroit's revitalization based on the constructive use of two abundant resources (vacant land and an unskilled workforce), numerous obstacles exist. Rendering its implementation a remote possibility, the obstacles are at least fourfold: practical, legal, psychological, and cultural. The practical obstacles include the difficulty in funding new enterprises, such as business cooperatives. Legal impediments include the absence of agriculture as a permitted use under the Detroit zoning code as well as a psychological barrier, namely, urban dwellers' distaste for farm work. In addition, it is extremely difficult to turn back from the twin cultural barriers posed by an entitlement state and by the American dream of a good job, a nice house and car, and a comfortable retirement.

In the context of for-profit entrepreneurship and nonprofit community endeavors, this book recommends that Detroiters try to embark on a difficult change. It urges them to go from a culture of entitlement where people expect a lifetime job at a large auto-related firm, for example, to a new culture of for-profit entrepreneurship and cooperative self-sufficiency, based on lifelong learning and the continual acquisition of new skills.

Building a broad-based entrepreneurial culture is not easy. For participants, the new culture involves taking a chance, launching a new project, whether a for-profit or a community-based endeavor; and if it fails, moving forward onto something else. But affordable rent, ample space, and a growing community of entrepreneurs may, despite long odds, facilitate risk-taking, apart from the traditional public sector or the big-firm corporate culture.

As the fiscal crisis at all levels of American government, federal, state, and local, grows ever deeper, some Detroiters may rethink the mindset built up over generations. If conditions get desperate enough, new ideas may come to fruition. For example, Spaniards, currently saddled with one of the industrialized world's highest jobless rates, have increasingly embraced bottom-up, self-help measures, such as local currencies, to supplement a fraying public safety net.[5]

Through the three pathways to revitalization developed in this book, as summarized in chapter 9's brief conclusion, which focuses on evaluating the odds of successful implementation, I hope that Detroit will once again be an urban area where residents feel safe, children thrive in quality schools, and people find gainful employment. However, Detroit's residents must find their own way.

Notes

1. Robert A. Beauregard, "Growth and Depopulation in the United States," in *Rebuilding America's Legacy Cities: New Directions for the Industrial Heartland,* ed. Alan Mallach (New York: American Assembly, 2012): 20–21.
2. For an analysis of the culture of distrust in economic development policy making and its impact on the formation of a community development corporation in Detroit enterprise zone planning, see Janice L. Bockmeyer, "A Culture of Distrust: The Impact of Local Political Culture on Participation in the Detroit EZ," *Urban Studies* 37:13 (December 2000): 2417–2440. For the importance of a culture of trust, see Francis Fukuyama, *Trust: The Social Virtues and the Creation of Prosperity* (New York: Free Press, 1995).
3. See, e.g., John P. Kretzmann and John L. McKnight, Building Communities from the Inside Out: A Path toward Finding and Mobilizing a Community's Assets (Evanston, IL: Institute for Policy Research Northwestern University, 1993). In contrast, Bruce Katz and Jennifer Bradley, "The Detroit Project: A plan for solving America's greatest urban disaster," *New Republic* 240:22 (December 2, 2009): 29–31, advocate a more traditional, top-down approach oriented around extensive public sector, especially federal government, involvement. See also Soji Adelaja, "Marshall Plan: Land/Place-Based Strategies for Detroit," July 14, 2010, Michigan State University Land Policy Institute, and Stephen Henderson, "One Leader Sees a Green Future for City," *Detroit Free Press,* February 15, 2009, EDP3.
4. Robert Skidelsky and Edward Skidelsky, *How Much Is Enough? Money and the Good Life* (New York: Other Press, 2012) question whether our current malaise stems from a love of money and material things, which fuel human insatiability and economic growth.
5. For a summary of locally oriented projects in Spain, involving tens of thousands of citizens and representing one of the largest experiments in social money in modern times, see Arianna Eunjung Cha, "A parallel euro-verse," *Washington Post,* August 28, 2012, A11, and Matt Moffett and Ilan Brat, "For Spain's Jobless, Time Equals Money," *Wall Street Journal,* August 27, 2012, A1.

I

Some Background and Context on Detroit

As Detroit strives to move forward and overcome its reputation as America's most dysfunctional big city, this part of the book provides some background and context for the next three parts. Chapter 1 gives a brief overview of the city's liabilities. Although Detroit faces many challenges, the city does not lack assets. Chapter 2 presents a succinct summary of its positive aspects.

1

Detroit's Challenges

Today, Detroit faces many challenges characteristic of advanced urban decay, including precipitous population losses; a shrinking tax base; too few jobs; an uneducated, unskilled workforce; fractured neighborhoods with many impoverished households; and unacceptably high levels of violent crime. Other aspects of urban disintegration, such as municipal budgetary shortfalls and inadequate public schools, are analyzed in chapters 3 and 5, respectively.

The totality of these liabilities poses significant, but not insurmountable, obstacles to Detroit's revitalization.

Racial Shifts and Massive Population Losses

Race and class underpin any analysis of Detroit's challenges and its potential prospects.[1] In the 1950s, shortly after Detroit's population peaked at 1.8 million, a white exodus from the city began. The suburban flight occurred, in part, as a result of the spread of highways built in the 1950s that opened accessibility to the suburbs; brought commuters in from beyond the city limits; but also disconnected neighborhoods in the city. The white trickle to the auto-oriented suburban sprawl in the Detroit metropolitan area became a flood beginning in 1967. Bitter racial tensions boiled over in the 1960s, culminating in the July 1967 race riots.[2] The police raid on an unlicensed club in a black neighborhood escalated into five days of rioting that took forty-three lives and resulted in the destruction of some 2,500 stores and other structures, beginning a legacy of burnt-out buildings and residences. The incident changed the city's racial composition almost immediately. As the result of racism and changing lifestyles, whites migrated from Detroit to the suburbs, in search of safety, more spacious homes, and bigger lot sizes; blacks, free from redlining by banks, migrated into all parts of Detroit, resulting in the creation of a racially segregated urban–suburban divide. The city did not want suburbanites telling it what to do; the safely ensconced suburbanites,

3

for the most part, lacked interest in helping with the city's growing burdens.

Roughly a century ago, in 1910, blacks accounted for 1.4 percent of Detroit's population. By 1960 and 1970, the percentage had grown, respectively, to some 29 percent and then to nearly 45 percent of the city's residents. By the mid-1970s, the city's black residents had become a majority. They accounted for about 83 (82.7) percent of the city's population of some 714,000 (713,777) people in 2010.[3]

Late in the first decade of this century, the middle-class black flight to the suburbs from Detroit grew, resulting in the city losing one-quarter of its population (some 237,500 people) between 2000 and 2010.[4] They threw in the towel frustrated by a legacy of municipal government corruption; failing public schools; high crime rates and insurance costs; a lack of quality public services; and plummeting residential property values triggered, in part, by an epidemic of mortgage foreclosures. Some 50,000 homes, about 20 percent of Detroit's residences, went into foreclosure during the Great Recession.[5] At the same time, the Detroit housing market collapsed. In February 2009, the median single-family residential sales price had dropped 42.6 percent from February 2008, to an unbelievable $5,737, only to rebound slightly to $7,100 by July 2009.[6] The collapse of housing prices, as one expert concludes, presents a number of negatives:

> Prices this low actually depress demand rather than increase it. While some may see low house prices as an asset, by making home ownership affordable to a larger spectrum of potential buyers, they actually create more problems than they solve. When existing houses sell for less than their replacement cost and have little likelihood of appreciating over time, developers have no incentive to build new houses on vacant land, and home buyers have no incentive to rehabilitate houses that have fallen into disrepair. Except for housing built or rehabilitated with public subsidies, the use of which . . . raises serious public policy issues, little or no replacement housing is being built in most shrinking cities.

> Despite low prices, prospective home buyers are few and far between. Many prefer to buy in nearby suburban communities—where house prices are slightly higher but still highly affordable—because of the greater likelihood of appreciation as well as real or perceived benefits in terms of safety and school quality. That, in turn, further depresses the demand for houses in urban neighborhoods and reduces home ownership rates, as more houses are bought by investors or speculators rather than by families planning to occupy the home they buy.[7]

4

Over the past fifty years, the more affluent left, first whites and more recently blacks, leaving poorer residents who face the twin barriers of race and class. At present, it is unclear whether the population free fall will continue, despite efforts to improve Detroit's public schools, analyzed in chapter 5, and the financial incentives to repopulate portions of the city, discussed in chapter 6. Seemingly, those who could leave have already departed, leaving a core population of some 500,000—poverty-stricken and poorly educated who cannot afford to exit—with a total of some 700,000 residents.

The population decline led to two negative consequences. First, the exodus of a huge tax base resulted in a decrease in public revenues to run the city. The massive number of vacant parcels and homes has led, according to one estimate, to some $173 million in lost property tax revenues annually.[8] Detroit also faced a decline in state revenue-sharing funds, which transfer a portion of state sales tax revenues to localities. Michigan apportions revenue sharing based on population. Funds come from two accounts. The state legislature now doles out funds from the Economic Vitality Incentive Program, with Detroit receiving some $120 million in fiscal year 2010–11, an annual reduction of $57 million from the previous statutory portion of state revenue sharing. There are also constitutional revenue-sharing funds, required under the state constitution, with Detroit obtaining some $46.9 million in fiscal year 2010–11.[9] Both streams of revenue sharing go into the city's general fund.

Second, in addition to eroding the tax base, the dramatic population losses decreased the demand for houses and land in the city. The number of vacant homes in Detroit more than doubled between 2000 and 2010. In 2000, vacant residences equaled about 10 percent of the city's housing stock. By 2010, more than one in five, nearly 23 percent of the homes in Detroit, were vacant—some 80,000 (79,725) housing units, 22.8 percent of the city's total housing stock of a little more than 349,000 (349,170) units.[10] Also, too much unproductive land exists, with more than 100,000 (100,719) parcels of land, public and private, 12.3 percent of the city's area, vacant.[11]

Abandoned, dilapidated single-family homes, some burnt-out, others graffiti-streaked or trashed by squatters, abound. Isolated, occupied residences as well as scattered clusters of houses are surrounded by empty lots strewn with rotting garbage, fast-food wrappers, and broken televisions. Incipient forests and fields of grass and weeds growing tall and lush in summer characterize Detroit's urban landscape. The derelict scene depresses property values and repels new investment. The blight also consists of deserted streets and empty storefronts with boarded-up windows and faded signs of long-closed stores and restaurants. More neighborhoods have become a wasteland, overrun with illegal drugs and crime. Dead zones detach the remaining, populated neighborhoods from each other. In sum, Detroit has gradually reverted to an urban prairie.[12]

A sprawling, auto-dominated city, with nearly 80 percent of its housing stock consisting of modest detached, wooden, hastily constructed single-family homes on 3,000-square-foot lots, Detroit finds it difficult to provide an adequate level of essential public services to a much smaller population. With some 700,000 people dispersed throughout the city's 139 square miles, as a low-density environment with a meager tax base, Detroit is simply too big for itself with so much of its expanse consisting of vacant, mostly untaxed land.

Deindustrialization and Deserted Office Buildings

Along with a massive population decline, a change in the city's racial composition, and strained relations with its suburbs, Detroit witnessed deindustrialization, as factory after factory and then office after office closed. Over the years, factories that once drove a mighty manufacturing base shuttered and warehouses were boarded up, leaving neighborhoods bereft of an economic base. From 1947 to 2007, manufacturing employment in Detroit plummeted from 338,400 to 22,962.[13] The huge job losses over the decades further reduced the municipal tax base. The city razed some of these empty factories and warehouses, leaving even more gaping holes in the urban landscape.

Over the years, many businesses left downtown, resulting in an abundance of abandoned or only partially occupied skyscrapers. Vacant or half-empty office buildings blight the downtown central business district. The citywide office vacancy rate soared from 17.1 percent in 2000, to 24 percent in 2004, and reached 27.8 percent in 2009. Downtown office vacancy rates hit nearly 32 percent by the end of the second quarter of 2010, only to decline slightly to 31.2 percent by the fourth quarter of 2011, and surge to 33.4 percent in the first quarter of 2012.[14] The number of empty downtown office buildings with at least five floors (or 10,000 square feet) stood at forty-nine at the end of 2011.[15] In downtown, sidewalks are cordoned off to protect pedestrians from falling chunks of building façade. Trees grow through water-damaged roofs. These empty (or nearly vacant) office buildings drain the city of potential taxes.

High Rates of Joblessness

Joblessness characterizes the city. In the depth of the Great Recession, Detroit's official unemployment rate reached 29 percent; its unofficial unemployment rate soared to nearly 50 percent.[16] The latter rate takes into account those who could not find a job; worked fewer hours than they wanted; worked part-time but wanted a full-time job; and discouraged workers who had stopped looking for work, having given up their job search for more than one year, and thus are not considered part of the labor force and are not counted as unemployed. In 2009, only 34 percent of Detroiters without a high school degree were employed; 52 percent were not even in the labor force.[17] Slightly under 50 (49.8) percent or some 174,000 Detroit residents, ages sixteen to sixty-four, do not work. Detroit's labor participation rate ranks as the lowest among America's big cities.[18] Absent extensive remediation, many of those out of the labor force may never find gainful, legal employment.

Several structural factors account for the city's extraordinarily high rate of unemployment, with the official 2011 employment rate at 19.9 percent.[19] When the auto industry crashed in 2008, no other industry existed to step forward to employ thousands of workers, who would have been delighted to make one-half of what they previously earned.

Urban sprawl limits access to jobs. Because large manufacturing plants were built outside the city, many low-income residents face isolation from suburban job opportunities. The Detroit area lacks a regional mass transit system; one in three households is without access to a car.[20] Although, the creation of a regional transit authority offers some hope in lessening the spatial mismatch.

Detroit faces a human capital challenge. Upwards of one-half (47 percent) of all Detroit adults, some 200,000 individuals, lack basic reading and writing skills needed to obtain and hold good-paying jobs that could sustain them and their families.[21] Of these adults, who are functionally illiterate, about one-half have a high school diploma or equivalent, evidence that the Detroit public school system has failed to educate students to a level that provides an adequate foundation for their future economic success. These human capital challenges may grow more pronounced in coming decades in view of the heightened skill requirements for the newly created jobs.

Endemic Poverty

Many Detroit residents are poverty-stricken. Some one-third (33.2 percent) of the city's residents earn incomes placing them below the federal poverty level, more than double the national average.[22] Another indicator of poverty in Detroit: the proportion of single-parent households with children under age eighteen, headed mainly by women, equals about two-thirds (23.9 percent out of 34.4 percent) of all family households with children in that age group.[23] Again, this is more than twice the national average. These single-parent households have lower incomes, lesser educational levels, and greater dependence on public assistance than two-parent families.[24]

Participation in government food and nutrition assistance programs provides another poverty indicator. About one in three Detroit households, some 98,000 households in 2010, relied on the Federal Supplemental Nutrition Assistance Program (SNAP) (formerly the Food Stamp Program) for help in buying food.[25] However, the SNAP benefit levels often are inadequate to purchase a range of healthy, fresh foods on a consistent basis. Another government program, the Federal Special Supplemental Nutrition Program for Women, Infants, and Children (WIC), provides supplemental foods, among other benefits, for low-income pregnant, breast-feeding, and non-breast-feeding women, their infants, and children up to the age five. About 35,000 eligible Detroit women, infants, and children participated monthly in the WIC program in 2010.[26]

School meals' programs benefit children from impoverished households. Through the National School Lunch Program more than one-half of all students in Detroit schools (public and charter) receive free or reduced-price lunches at school. Somewhat fewer also receive free breakfasts under the Federal School Breakfast Program.[27]

In sum, Detroit presents significant labor market challenges in terms of unemployment, labor force participation, educational levels, and poverty, along with job sprawl. A mismatch exists between available jobs and workers' skills. Many lack the skills requisite for the available jobs, currently[28] and likely in the future.

Despite these challenges—presenting significant but not insurmountable obstacles to Detroit's revitalization—the city possesses numerous assets as discussed in the next chapter.

Notes

1. See generally Thomas J. Sugrue, *The Origins of the Urban Crisis: Race and Inequality in Postwar Detroit* (Princeton, NJ: Princeton University, 1996). See also Thomas J. Sugrue, "A Dream Still Deferred," *New York Times*, March 27, 2011, Section WK, 11. For grim narratives of Detroit's descent, see Scott Martelle, *Detroit: A Biography* (Chicago: Chicago Review Press, 2012) and Ze'ev Chafets, *Devil's Night and Other True Tales* (New York: Random House, 1990). See generally Heather Ann Thompson, *Whose Detroit? Politics, Labor, and Race in a Modern American City* (Ithaca, NY: Cornell University, 2001); Reynolds Farley, Sheldon Danziger, Harry J. Holzer, *Detroit Divided* (New York: Russell Sage, 2000); Robert Conot, *American Odyssey* (New York: William Morrow, 1974). For the economic and social changes that occurred in Detroit and its metropolitan area in the 1960s and 1970s, see Joe T. Darden et al., *Detroit: Race and Uneven Development* (Philadelphia: Temple University, 1987).

2. Sidney Fine, *Violence in the Model City: The Cavanagh Administration, Race Relations, and the Detroit Riot of 1967* (Ann Arbor: University of Michigan, 1989), 155–247.

3. The statistics in this paragraph were derived from the US Census Bureau <www.census.gov>. See generally Kate Linebaugh, "Detroit Population Crashes," *Wall Street Journal*, March 23, 2011, A3, and Katharine Q. Seelye, "Detroit Census Figures Confirm a Grim Desertion Like no Other," *New York Times*, March 23, 2011, A11. See also Kami Pothukuchi, The Detroit Food System Report 2009–2010, Detroit Food Policy Council, May 15, 2011, 23–24, and Kristen Kasinsky, "Detroit: Built for the Road Ahead?," *Michigan Sociological Review* 23 (Fall 2009): 160–176, at 162.

4. Alex P. Kellogg, "Black Flight Hits Detroit," *Wall Street Journal*, June 5, 2012, A1. For a quantitative and theoretical assessment of population loss in large US cities, see Robert A. Beauregard, "Urban population loss in historical perspective: United States, 1820–2000," *Environment and Planning* A 41:3 (January 1, 2009): 514–528. See also Robert A. Beauregard, "Growth and Depopulation in the United States," in *Rebuilding America's Legacy Cities: New Directions for the Industrial Heartland*, ed. Alan Mallach (New York: American Assembly, 2012), 1–24.

5. John Gallagher, "City's fight against vacant lots gets tougher," *Detroit Free Press*, September 29, 2009, A1, and John Gallagher, *Reimaging Detroit: Opportunities for Redefining an American City* (Detroit: Wayne State University, 2010), 119.

6. Greta Quest, "Foreclosures spur home sales," *Detroit Free Press*, March 10, 2009, B3, and Michael M. Phillips, "In One Home, a Mighty City's Rise and Fall," *Wall Street Journal*, September 26, 2009, A1.

7. Alan Mallach, "Depopulation, Market Collapse, and Property Abandonment: Surplus Land and Buildings in Legacy Cities," in *Rebuilding America's Legacy Cities*, 93.

8. The Detroit Works Project (DWP), Who will live here? Additional Population Reduces Individual Tax Burden, n.d.

9. City of Detroit, Office of the Auditor General, Analysis of the Mayor's 2012–2013 Proposed Budget, May 8, 2012, 2–4. To be eligible to receive revenue sharing under the Economic Vitality Incentive Program, a locality must fulfill specific requirements for Accountability and Transparency, Consolidation of Services, and Employee Compensation. Public Act 63 of 2011 (Section 951) and State of Michigan, Department of Treasury, Economic Vitality Incentive Program (EVIP) – Incentive Program <www.michigan.gov/treasury/0,1607,7-121-1751_2197-259414--,00.html> (June 29, 2012).

10. The statistics in this paragraph are from Christine MacDonald, "Vacant homes stoke city woes," *Detroit News*, December 26, 2011, A3, and John Gallagher, "Vacancy rate up as 1 in 5 Detroit homes is empty," *Detroit Free Press*, March 23, 2011, C4. See generally, US Government Accountability Office, Vacant Properties: Growing Number Increases Communities Costs and Challenges, GAO-12-34, November 2011, for a report on vacant properties nationwide. For a study of vacancies in a Detroit neighborhood, see Eric Dueweke, "Case Study: Vacancy in Detroit: One Nine-Block Area" in *Rebuilding America's Legacy Cities*, 111–114.

11. DWP, Phase One: Research and Priorities: Policy Audit Topic: Public Land Disposition Policies and Procedures, December 22, 2010, 3.4 (The Public Land). See also Monica Davey, "Detroit Starts to Think Smaller, Literally," *New York Times*, April 6, 2011, A14.

12. For a description of Detroit's return to nature see, e.g., Rebecca Solnit, "Detroit Arcadia: Exploring the post-American landscape," *Harper's* 315:1886 (July 2007): 65–73. See also Mallach, "Depopulation, Market Collapse, and Property Abandonment," 94–98.

13. City of Detroit, Proposed 2012–2013 Budget, Executive Summary (Proposed 2012–2013 Budget), E3 (Manufacturing Sector in Detroit City since 1947).

14. Grubb & Ellis, Office Market Trends Q4 2011 United States, 2012 and Grubb & Ellis, 2012 Forecast Edition Office Trends Report—Fourth Quarter 2011, Detroit, MI. See also Bryce G. Hoffman and Louis Aguilar, "Chrysler makes downtown move," *Detroit News*, April 26, 2012, A1; Louis Aguilar, "Quicken move inspires hope," *Detroit News*, July 15, 2010, B4; and Louis Aguilar, "48 vacant buildings blight downtown," *Detroit News*, August 17, 2009, A1.

15. Louis Aguilar, "Despite progress, vacant buildings dot downtown," *Detroit News*, December 5, 2011, A1.

16. Proposed 2012–2013 Budget, E5 (Annual Civilian Unemployment Rates % by Place of Residence). See also Daniel Howes, "Michigan 'facts' [sic] a dismal prospect," *Detroit News*, December 17, 2009, B4, and Mike Wilkinson, "Nearly half of Detroit's workers are unemployed," *Detroit News*, December 16, 2009, A1.

17. Initiative for a Competitive Inner City (ICIC), Phase One: Research and Priorities: Policy Audit Topic: Urban & Regional Economy (Urban and Regional Economy), DWP, December 16, 2010, 1.3 (Challenges and Opportunities: Labor Force Status across Large U.S. Cities), 3.1 (Overview: Total Labor Market: Percent Employment Status: Population Aged 16–64), and

3.2 (Workforce Benchmarks: Employment Status and Not in Labor Force Status).

18. John Gallagher and Jeff Seidel, "Jobs seen as the key to jump-start the city," *Detroit Free Press*, April 8, 2012, A1.

19. 2012–2013 Proposed Budget, E5, and Gallagher and Seidel, "Jobs seen."

20. ICIC, Urban & Regional Economy, 2.1 (Access to Private Vehicles). See also Elizabeth Kneebone, Job Sprawl Revisited: The Changing Geography of Metropolitan Employment, Metro Economy Series for the Metropolitan Policy Program at Brookings, April 2009, 8 (Table 2. Most Centralized and Decentralized Metro Areas by Employment Share, by Metro Area Employment Size, 2006), 12 (Table 5. 98 Metro Areas by Type of Change in the Spatial Location of Employment, 1998 to 2006), Appendix A. (Change in the Geographic Distribution of Jobs, 98 Metro Areas, 1998 to 2006); Louis Aguilar, "Area lags in jobs served by public transit," *Detroit Free Press*, July 12, 2012, C1; Louis Aguilar, "Detroit area tops in job sprawl," *Detroit News*, April 6, 2009, A1.

21. Detroit Regional Workforce Fund, Addressing Detroit's Basic Skills Crisis, n.d., 2, 5; National Institute for Literacy, The State of Literacy in America: Estimates at the Local, State, and National Levels, Washington, DC, 1998, The State of Literacy in America Level 1 Literacy Rates by State, Michigan, Detroit City, n.p.; DWP, Where Will People Work? <www.detroitworksproject.com/opportunities-challenge/where-will-people-work> (March 29, 2012). See also Katherine Yung, "Detroit lacking services for job skills, study finds," *Detroit Free Press*, May 8, 2011, B1, but see E.D. Kain, "Detroit Literacy Numbers Questionable," Forbes.com, May 6, 2011 (November 8, 2011).

22. Detroit (City) Quick Facts from US Census Bureau <www.quickfacts.census.gov/qfd/states/26/2622000.html> (November 29, 2011) and ICIC, Urban & Regional Economy, 1.1 (The Case for Change: Social Conditions in Detroit).

23. US Census Bureau, American Fact Finder, Profile of General Population and Housing Characteristics: 2010, 2010 Demographic Profile Data, Detroit city, Michigan (November 29, 2011). See also, DWP, Urban & Regional Economy, 1.1 (The Case for Change: Social Conditions in Detroit).

24. Lewis D. Solomon, *Cycles of Poverty and Crime in America's Inner Cities* (New Brunswick, NJ: Transaction, 2012, 14.) The dysfunctionality of single-parent families, even controlling for income, contributes to a host of social ills: juvenile delinquency and crime; failing or dropping out of school; engaging in early and promiscuous sexual activity, thereby repeating the cycle of nonmarital births; developing drug and alcohol problems; and suffering emotional or behavioral problems requiring mental health care. Children born outside of marriage generally face significant disadvantages in education achievement and personal growth. They have generally lower cognitive and emotional development, greater problems with self-control, and are often diagnosed as hyperactive. Ibid., 14–15.

25. US Census Bureau, American Fact Finder, Food Stamps/SNAP, 2010 American Community Survey 1-year Estimates.

26. Detroit Food System Report 2009–2010, 10, 47.

27. Food Research and Action Center, School Breakfast in America's Big Cities: School Year 2010–2011, 10 (Table 1: Average Daily Participation

(ADP) for Low-Income Students in Lunch and Breakfast for SY 2009–10 and SY 2010–11, 10, 48. See also Detroit Food System Report 2009–2010, 10, 48.

28. Conor Dougherty, "Gap Hurts Job Hunters," *Wall Street Journal*, August 29, 2012, A3, and Jonathan Rothwell, "Education, Job Openings, and Unemployment in Metropolitan America," Metropolitan Policy Program at Brookings, August 2012.

2

Detroit's Substantial Assets

Despite the numerous challenges Detroit faces, it is a legacy city with a rich historical heritage, an excellent location, and many significant assets. Geography favors Detroit. The Great Lakes international waterways make it accessible. The city has extensive highway and rail systems enabling it to be a gateway not only to the Midwest but also throughout the United States. A major international airport, the Detroit Metropolitan Wayne County Airport, located in a nearby suburb, affords excellent domestic and overseas connections.

It has fine hotel accommodations and restaurants that attract millions of tourists annually. The city hosts every major professional sports team. It possesses two state-of-the-art sports stadiums, Ford Field for football and Comerica Park for baseball.

As a result of depopulation and the real estate crash, discussed in chapter 1, property is inexpensive by US urban standards. The city offers low-cost housing and inexpensive office and factory space. Creative types, such as artists and musicians, find affordable living and work space.

It has numerous physical assets, including historic buildings and a number of tree-lined, vibrant, well-maintained, stable neighborhoods, although these are scattered across the city. It has a strong, clearly identifiable urban core. Its downtown is physically intact. Mixed-use areas near downtown, such as Midtown and Corktown, contain clusters of nonindustrial employment, cultural activity, and diverse residential areas with respect to housing type and price range. In particular, as discussed in chapter 6, Midtown has become a vibrant community.

In addition to enjoying an abundance of fresh water, its rejuvenated riverfront, the Detroit Riverwalk,[1] is spectacular. The urban waterway provides a visual amenity and serves as a magnet for those who want to stroll, jog, or bike in a park setting. The Dequindre Cut, a 1.3-mile, below-grade, paved pedestrian and bicycle pathway, connects the riverfront to the city's historic Eastern Market District. The city's renowned

Eastern Market, located just east of downtown, spans some six blocks and hosts hundreds of open-air farmers' market stalls, where Detroiters have looked for fresh produce and meat since 1891.[2] It also is a food district where more than 250 independent sellers and merchants engage in processing, wholesaling, and retailing mostly local food, among other nearby products.

It has valuable human capital, including governmental, business, nonprofit, and neighborhood leaders as well as ordinary citizens, who want to make their city a better place in which to live and work. It has a rich reservoir of creativity and innovation reflected in areas as diverse as music, for example, Motown, and energy-saving technology.

Detroit's Anchor Institutions

Detroit contains many anchor institutions. Its more than twenty medical centers, including the Children's Hospital of Michigan, the Henry Ford Health System, the Detroit Medical Center, and the Karmanos Cancer Institute, not only provide nationally recognized care to patients and employment to thousands but also generate private sector activities in biomedicine and health care. It has two prominent universities, Wayne State University (WSU) and University of Detroit Mercy, and a leading art school, the College for Creative Studies (CCS). Both WSU and CCS have become active agents in promoting Detroit's rebirth. Its leading arts and culture institutions include the Detroit Institute of Arts (DIA)—an encyclopedic visual arts museum, covering all genres, cultures, and timeframes, which the city transferred to nonprofit ownership in 1998—the Detroit Symphony Orchestra (DSO), and the Charles H. Wright Museum of African American History.

High culture in art and music serve as a public benefit, providing jobs and luring talented professionals. However, in the twenty-first century, attendance at these venues is shrinking and audiences are aging. Arts education represents an endangered species marked by the disappearance of art and music from the public schools. Live music faces fierce competition in the Internet and digital music.

The Great Recession and the downsizing of Detroit's corporate landscape resulted in falling business support to nonprofit organizations. Sagging ticket sales, the evaporation of public-sector funding, and wealthy donors' inability to make up the difference led to financial crises for the DIA and the DSO, two old-line Detroit cultural institutions. For example, the DIA reduced its operating budget from

$35 million to $25 million in 2011 and eliminated nearly 20 percent of its workforce. Labor issues compounded the DSO's plight. A disastrous six-month musicians' strike dragged on from October 2010 to April 2011, all but wiping out the 2010–11 season. Foreshadowing the 2012 developments with respect to municipal employees, ultimately, the strike was settled on terms highly favorable to management, with the musicians accepting a huge (23 percent) pay cut.[3]

At present, it is unclear whether the DSO will retain its historic place among the nation's orchestras.[4] It is trying to cultivate wealthy, younger patrons as donors and board members, with 2011 marked by DSO's impressive fund-raising effort.[5] Funded by a five-year (2011–15), $2.5 million grant from The Kresge Foundation, the DSO has embarked on a campaign to extend the reach of classical music with a menu of community concerts across the Detroit metropolitan area.[6] Most importantly, in May 2012, the DSO and five banks reached a deal that erased some $54 million in debt.

With voters approving a tri-county (Wayne, Oakland, and Macomb) ten-year real estate tax increase in August 2012, the DIA was saved from devastating budget cuts, if not closure.[7] In asking for public funding, the DIA sweetened the pill with an imaginative free-admission plan for county residents. It is unclear, however, whether the DIA will be able to build a substantial endowment to ensure its long-term financial viability.

With its major cultural institutions facing difficult times, the "action" has shifted to individual artists (examined in chapter 7), cultural entrepreneurs, such as gallery owners, and smaller institutions, such as the Museum of Contemporary Art Detroit (MOCAD), housed in a former auto dealership.[8] MOCAD, which opened in 2006, with its deliberately raw interior and an exterior painted with graffiti, has helped foster the growth of one of the nation's most thriving arts' communities.

In addition to these anchor institutions, Detroit has experienced newly emerging business clusters. As discussed in chapter 6, led by Daniel R. (Dan) Gilbert, the billionaire chairman of Quicken Loans, Inc., businesses are injecting new people, vitality, and capital into the city's life. These firms lend credibility to Detroit eschewing its one-industry automobile-town "rap" and striving to become a hub of high tech, health care, higher education, and entrepreneurship. These business leaders want to transform the city, *à la* Pittsburgh, through its anchor health care and higher education institutions and build an information technology center. With artists paying little for distressed residences and turning them into creative installations, the city is trying to rebrand itself as a place nurturing creativity, building on the historic base of its world-class cultural offerings.

The Role of Foundations

Foundations will play a vital role in twenty-first century Detroit. Although foundations, their leaders, and funds cannot solve all of the city's problems, nonprofit dollars in the right places can, at least, get things rolling, particularly with respect to public-private partnerships. In the municipal government arena, foundations can support public-sector capacity building through grants, training programs, and partnerships. Funding much-needed personnel, especially in view of Detroit's fiscal austerity, as analyzed in chapter 3, philanthropic resources can augment depleted staff, provide technical expertise, and support strategic planning efforts.

Today, Detroit's nonprofit funders are divvying up projects according to their respective missions. They are finding new ways to collaborate.[9] For example, the New Economy Initiative for Southeast Michigan, a $100 million, eight-year initiative effort of ten foundations, local and national, works as one group to ramp up metro Detroit's economy by creating a strong entrepreneurial ecosystem, thereby helping move Michigan beyond its reliance on the auto industry.[10] Building on Detroit's philanthropic base and the skills of its existing workforce, the initiative strives to improve regional coordination and the effectiveness of the workforce system through collaborative strategies linking workforce and economic development and education.

Detroit is blessed with at least eight major, locally based foundations and several national foundations with Michigan roots. The key local foundations include The Kresge Foundation, Skillman Foundation, Community Foundation for Southeast Michigan (Community Foundation), Max M. and Marjorie S. Fisher Foundation, Hudson-Webber Foundation, McGregor Fund, Charles Stewart Mott Foundation, and the W.K. Kellogg Foundation (Kellogg Foundation). The national foundations include the Ford Foundation (New York based) and the John S. and James L. Knight Foundation (Miami based). All of these foundations are interested in and provide funds to support Detroit's revival.

The Kresge Foundation, a $3.1 billion fund, based in a bucolic farmhouse in suburban Troy, Michigan, exemplifies how philanthropy can provide both seed money and imagination.[11] It was founded in 1924 by Sebastian S. Kresge, who launched the Kresge (now Kmart) Corp., and is now led by Richard (Rip) Rapson, its president and CEO since 2006. In recent years, Kresge has invested well in excess of $100 million in Detroit's transformation. Concentrating its resources in a specific urban area, nearly 15 (14.4) percent of its total grants in 2011 went to Detroit.[12] It is willing to take risks; collaborate with other foundations and various public-private partners around which the public and the for-profit private sectors can build; and piggyback on existing (and proposed) economic development projects. According to Rapson: "Philanthropy has emerged as the sector best able to provide the long-term vision and short-term investment of capital the city needs to right itself."[13]

Kresge's Detroit Program represents a comprehensive, multi-part community-development effort, called Re-imagining Detroit 2020, aimed at enhancing the city's long-term economic, social, and cultural fabric.[14] The program includes strengthening Detroit's neighborhoods and its downtown; promoting arts and culture; advancing entrepreneurial economic development; and enhancing the natural environment.

Rapson has an overarching vision for the city.[15] He wants more emphasis on and more investment in strong neighborhoods, ones clustered near main roads radiating from downtown, and healthier enclaves, such as Boston–Edison. Conversely, he sees weaker neighborhoods, blighted and depopulated, as ripe for restoring the natural ecology, including planting new forests and unearthing buried creeks, as Detroit slowly returns to nature.

An early backer of the Detroit Works Project, analyzed in chapter 4, Kresge funded data-collections efforts and the salary of Toni L. Griffin, a noted urban planner. However, the foundation stopped its funding at the start of 2011 because of disagreements with city hall over the role of consultants in the project, only to resume funding in December 2011. It also supported data-collection efforts and augmented the salary of Detroit Public Schools' Emergency Financial Manager.[16]

As examined in chapter 6, Kresge pledged $35 million to spark the $500 million development of the M-1 Light Rail transit line along Woodward Avenue,[17] the city's spine, which would have created an urban coherence and help jump-start economic activity around each station. In the end, the ill-fated project never was implemented.

Kresge has sought to build Detroit's cultural environment by providing operating support to large, medium, and small grassroots organizations in the performing, visual, and literary arts and to arts-infrastructure groups, as well as backing other arts projects, including individual artists, as discussed in chapter 7.[18] The three-year (2009–11)

$8.8 million commitment by the foundation provided a critical cash infusion to arts groups that struggled during the Great Recession.

To implement its ecological vision, Kresge has funded various projects, in whole or in part with other foundations.[19] From 2002 to 2008, a series of Kresge grants totaling $50 million provided funding for the Detroit Riverwalk, a $140 million project that included backing by the Community Foundation and the Kellogg Foundation. Through the nonprofit Detroit Riverfront Conservancy, the project reclaimed and opened a landscaped walkway, initially three miles in length, along the Detroit River. Kresge helped fund local greenways, such as the Dequindre Cut, as part of the Community Foundation's greenways initiative, the Detroit Greenway Coalition. Kresge is also largely responsible for the redevelopment of the city's Eastern Market.

Despite the best efforts of foundation leaders, many locals, however, perceive foundations and their individual and collective energy, as exemplified by Rapson, as a current (as well as a potential) power grab by outsiders.[20] Viewed as knowing better than residents, suspicions exist that foundations will dominate many aspects of public-sector decision making. Because they have money to fund projects in an era of governmental fiscal austerity, some locals fear foundations will not allow any meaningful community input in efforts such as the Detroit Works Project, thereby resulting in a takeover of residents' destiny.

After providing an overview of Detroit's challenges and assets, we can turn and analyze efforts to overcome the city's fiscal crisis, revamp its public sector and schools, and engage in land-use planning. The obstacles Detroit faces in these endeavors are also examined.

Notes

1.   The Detroit Riverfront Conservancy, "Vision and Mission" <www.detroitriverfront.org/drc/vision> (December 8, 2011). See also Nolan Finley, "Riverfront vision becomes reality," *Detroit News*, November 24, 2011, B1, and Betsy Hemming, "The Detroit Riverfront Conservancy: A Public-Private Partnership Striving to Reclaim the Detroit River," *Golden Gate University Law Review* 35:3 (Spring 2005): 395–410.

2.   Eastern Market Corp., "Market Historic" <www.detroiteasternmarket.com/page.php.?=1&5=58> (June 4, 2012). See also Rene Wisely, "Eastern Market blossoms," *Detroit News*, April 21, 2012, A1; Louis Aguilar, "Eastern Market keeps evolving," *Detroit News*, February 3, 2012, A11; Louis Aguilar, "Eastern

Market gets a lift," *Detroit News*, January 12, 2012, B6; John Gallagher, "Renovations start at Eastern Market," *Detroit Free Press* , January 12, 2012, A8; John Gallagher, "How Eastern Market reinvented itself," *Detroit Free Press*, June 26, 2010, A5; Jennifer Youssef, "Eastern Market helps entrepreneurs flourish," *Detroit* News, October 9, 2009, B6.

3. Detroit Symphony Orchestra (DSO), Press Release, "Musicians of the Detroit Symphony Orchestra Ratify New Contract," April 8, 2011 <www.detroitsymphony.com/page.aspx?page_id=703> (December 28, 2011). See also Terry Teachout, "A Symphonic Suicide Attempt," *Commentary* 131:5 (May 2011): 54–57 and Daniel J. Wakin, "Detroit Symphony Returns to a Giddy Reception," *New York Times*, April 11, 2011, C1.

4. See, e.g., Michael Hodges and Lawrence B. Johnson, "Arts venues aim for comeback," *Detroit News*, December 9, 2011, A1, and Mark Stryker, "Who will save the arts?," *Detroit Free Press*, March 28, 2011, J4.

5. Michael Hodges, "DSO fund-raising closes out 2011 with a big finish," *Detroit News*, January 18, 2012, A7.

6. DSO, Press Release, "Detroit Symphony Orchestra Announces Metro Detroit Concert Initiative," October 28, 2011 <blog.dso.org/2011/10> (December 28, 2011). See also Lawrence B. Johnson, "DSO and Mozart take a neighborhood spin," *Detroit News*, January 26, 2012, M15; Lawrence B. Johnson, "DSO hits the neighborhoods," *Detroit News*, January 5, 2012, M7; Daniel Okrent, Karen Dybis, Kristy Erdobi, "And the Band Played On," *Time* 176:1 (July 5, 2010): 69–71.

7. Terry Teachout, "Why Arts Managers Short of Cash Are Looking to Detroit," *Wall Street Journal*, August 17, 2012, D8; Patricia Cohen, "Suburban Taxpayers Vote to Support Detroit Museum," *New York Times*, August 9, 2012, C1; Mark Stryker, "DIA millage gets big support in Wayne and Oakland, but victory slim in Macomb," *Detroit Free Press*, August 8, 2012, A1; Lauren Abdel-Razzaq, "DIA tax easily passes in Wayne, Oakland," *Detroit News*, August 8, 2012, A9; Matthew Doland, "Detroit Museum Seeks Tax Boost," *Wall Street Journal*, August 7, 2012, A3; Judith H. Dobrzynski, "Where There's a Mill, There's a Way," *Wall Street Journal*, August 2, 2012, D6; David Runk, "Detroit art museum makes pitch for voter support," *Washington Post*, July 22, 2012, E5; Steve Pardo, "Wayne Co. paves way for DIA tax vote," *Detroit News*, March 30, 2012, A8; Laura Berman, "DIA frets its art may be at risk," *Detroit News*, February 13, 2012, A1; Joel Kurth, "DIA explores regional tax for museum operations," *Detroit News*, February 3, 2012, A1.

8. Martin F. Kohn, "A Good Year for Art with an Edge," *Detroit Free Press*, October 29, 2007, FTR1; Keri Guten Cohen, "MOCAD," *Detroit Free Press*, December 8, 2006, FTR6; Martin F. Kohn, "An Unpredictable Kind of Museum," *Detroit Free Press*, October 22, 2006, FTR1; Michael H. Hodges, "Gotta have (modern) art," *Detroit News*, October 19, 2006, E1.

9. See, e.g., Laura Berman and Christine MacDonald, "Foundations seek new foundation of Detroit," *Detroit News*, March 26, 2010, A1, and Stephanie Strom, "As Detroit Struggles, Foundations Adjust," *New York Times*, March 22, 2009, A14.

10. Laura Berman, "10 local philanthropies work together to boost the economy," *Detroit News*, March 26, 2010, A11, and Sherri Welch, "Building foundations," *Crain's Detroit Business* 27:344, August 22, 2011, S11. See also Robert

Giloth and Jillien Meier, "Human Capital and Legacy Cities," in *Rebuilding America's Legacy Cities: New Directions for the Industrial Heartland,* ed. Alan Mallach (New York: American Assembly, 2012), 214.

11.   For background on The Kresge Foundation see The Kresge Foundation (Kresge) "About Us," <www.kresge.org/about-us> (November 22, 2011). See also Michael H. Hodges, "Dime-store entrepreneur started Kresge Foundation," *Detroit News,* June 30, 2009, A7, and Kresge, Press Release, "Detroit News Heralds Kresge as a Local Leader for Urban Revitalization," August 5, 2009 <www.kresge.org/news/detroit-news-heralds-kresge-local-leader for urban-revitalization> (December 8, 2011).

12.   The Foundation Center, The Kresge Foundation, US Giving by Recipient Type and Giving in Michigan by Recipient Type, 2011 <www.foundationcenter. org/grantmakers/index.php?source=recip&gmkey=KRES002> (May 17, 2012). See also Michael H. Hodges, "Troy nonprofit steps up gifts and auto sector retreats," *Detroit News,* June 30, 2009, A1.

13.   Quoted in Matthew Dolan, "Revival Bid Pits Detroit vs. Donor," *Wall Street Journal,* July 2–3, 2011, A1.

14.   Kresge, "Detroit" <www.kresge.org/programs/detroit> (November 22, 2011).

15.   Dolan, "Revival."

16.   Ibid. See also Laura Berman, "In aiding Detroit, Kresge head learns impatience is not virtue," *Detroit News,* July 15, 2011, A1.

17.   Dolan, "Revival."

18.   Kresge, Press Release, "Kresge Announces $8.8 Million Commitment to Metro Detroit Arts Community," October 15, 2009 <www.kresge.org/news/ kresge-announces-88-million-commitment-metro-detroit-arts> (December 8, 2011) and Kresge, "Area Arts and Culture Organizations to Benefit from $6 million in Grant Assistance," June 16, 2007 <www.kresge.org/news/ area-arts-and-culture-organizations-benefit-6-million-grant> (December 8, 2011).

19.   Kresge, "Detroit Riverfront Conservancy and Detroit Greenway Coalition" <www.kresge.org/detroit-riverfront-conservancy-and-detroit-greenway-coalition> (December 8, 2011).

20.   Berman and MacDonald, "Foundations."

II

Surmounting Detroit's Fiscal Crisis and Revamping Its Municipal Public Sector and Public School District

Detroit's public sector faces three Herculean tasks, each of which presents an obstacle to its revitalization. First, as discussed in chapter 3, the city must regain its fiscal sanity. Detroit must ensure that its revenues match (if not exceed) its expenditures, while providing essential public services, such as public safety. At the same time, as analyzed in chapter 4, Detroit must rightsize its public services to match its sprawling but shrinking population. Third, as considered in chapter 5, to retain and attract residents, Detroit must not only assure the financial viability of its public schools but also significantly improve their academic performance.

The year 2009 marked an important turning point in beginning to meet these three challenges. In January 2009, the Michigan governor appointed an emergency financial manager for the beleaguered Detroit Public School (DPS) district. Thereafter, the DPS system began to turn around financially and provide children with a sound knowledge base for their future success. As analyzed in chapter 5, it appears probable that the district will continue on the path to financial viability. At present, it is possible that the academic performance of K–12 students will improve, as well as the high school graduation rate. These are difficult tasks resting, in part, on parents taking a greater interest in their children's education and the opposition of the teachers' union to academic changes.

Also in 2009, a political reawakening occurred in city hall, starting with Detroit's new mayor, David (Dave) Bing (D), and city council president, Charles Pugh (D). Bing, a basketball legend and business

21

leader (the owner of The Bing Group, a now defunct steel distribution company), became a politician.[1] Promising change and a new approach to governing, Bing won a special election in May 2009 to fill the balance of an unexpired mayoral term—following municipal scandals and eventual criminal indictments, and a general election in November 2009—for a four-year term beginning in January 2010. Bing came into office with a city council majority that shared his penchant for competence and a change-minded agenda.[2]

Until it was too late, however, Bing and his team often spurned the efforts of several more realistic council members to craft a more aggressive response to Detroit's growing financial crisis, by dramatically reining in spending. City officials had allowed budget deficits to accumulate by more than $100 million annually between 2005 and 2010, adding some $500 million in new debt during this period to pay Detroit's bills, ultimately burying the city in more than $5 billion of debt.[3] In fairness, bringing municipal finances under control by reshaping the city's labor-management relationship proved a difficult, if not impossible, task. As developed in chapter 3, with the appointment of an emergency manager in March 2013, it appears probable that the city will be on the road to financial viability and may avoid bankruptcy. However, the specter of bankruptcy looms on the horizon for Detroit, particularly in view of falling municipal revenues.

Bing also sought to achieve an equally tough objective: concentrating public services in the city's more densely populated, more viable neighborhoods. Here Bing floated a blueprint for future land use that evidenced leadership, regardless of the political consequences. However, as examined in chapter 4, his drive to reshape the city to focus the delivery of needed services for a good quality of life and avoid drastic across-the-board cuts that would drive out more residents petered out in the effort to avoid insolvency. A 2011 short-term action plan, implemented in three demonstration areas, only achieved modest gains. The 2012 long-term plan, the Detroit Strategic Framework Plan, succeeded in addressing and overcoming a legacy of suspicion and distrust involving planning efforts and gaining a consensus that Detroit as a smaller place could be a better place. Beyond these achievements, the plan will likely sit on the shelf, with low odds for comprehensive implementation, at least for the foreseeable future. Also, the plan suffered from a notable deficiency: the lack of any type of funding mechanism. However, The Kresge Foundation pledged $100 million over the next five years to assist in implementing the plan.

3

Struggling to Deal with Detroit's Fiscal Crisis

In April 2012, Detroit and Michigan entered into a strategy for dealing with the city's fiscal mismanagement and its ever-deepening financial troubles. With the municipality swimming in red ink and facing the looming specter of insolvency, the city and the state entered into a Financial Stability Agreement. Prior to mid-2012—despite shedding public-sector jobs, cutting pay, trimming benefits, and curbing services— the city could never reduce its operations to match its shrinking tax base, in large measure, because of municipal employee unions' intransigency. This chapter analyzes budgetary events leading up to the agreement and its impact, particularly with respect to the city's unionized employees. However, the agreement proved inadequate. It is probable that the March 2013 appointment of an emergency manager will put Detroit on the path to financial solvency—fixing the city's budget by balancing revenue with expenses, while enabling the municipality to provide essential public services to its residents, although bankruptcy remains a possibility.

The Approaching Financial Storm

Mayor Bing spent his first three years in office largely focused on Detroit's financial crisis and restructuring municipal public services. Stabilizing the city's financial health and restoring fiscal sanity by increasing revenues, where possible, and bringing spending under control, served as his highest priorities, along with establishing (and maintaining) a safe and secure city and facilitating the creation of private-sector jobs.

Although Bing inherited a city in a distressed financial condition, after years of mismanagement and an extended period of fiscal imbalance, he failed to turn around Detroit's persistent financial problems. He did not act decisively to stop the slide into insolvency by eliminating its structural budget deficits. He never persuaded a city council majority to implement an aggressive financial and operational restructuring plan.

Bing, a good person, kept trying to do the right thing, but he faced recalcitrant city employee unions and could not keep his appointees from spending beyond their departmental budgets. For his first two years in office, he also was unable to keep his management team, which often seemed adrift, together. There were scores of departures of top-level aides, making building momentum difficult. The in-fighting led to what one journalist described as a "back-stabbing free-for-all."[4] In the context of a battle of personalities, Bing consolidated power in a few top aides. He rarely listened to those outside his tight, frequently changing group of advisers.

A large measure of stability returned in June 2011, when Bing brought back Kirk J. Lewis as his chief of staff.[5] Several months before, in March 2011, Lewis left city hall, when Bing objected to Lewis's candidacy as emergency manager of the Detroit Public School District. When he returned, Lewis ran city hall's day-to-day operations, with major department heads reporting directly through him to the mayor. He also sought to improve Bing's frayed relations with the city council, gradually forged a viable leadership team, and urged the mayor to be more visible in the community.

Despite the chaos in his management team from 2009 to mid-2011, Bing made some progress on the financial front. Bing inherited an accumulated $332 ($331.9) million budget deficit as of June 30, 2009, that he reduced to $197 ($196.6) million by the end of June two years later,[6] only to see it balloon to about $265 million in mid-2012. To decrease the city's accumulated deficit, Bing increased its revenues, borrowed money, and reduced expenses.

To bolster revenues, in June 2011 Bing obtained $20 million from an escrow fund related to Detroit Edison's (a subsidiary of DTE Energy) purchase of electricity generated by a resource recovery project at Detroit's municipal trash incinerator, after the Michigan Public Service Commission approved the escrow release. The fund had been held in escrow for years, following the sale of a city incinerator. The city also received $55 million in delinquent property tax receipts from Wayne County.[7] In the face of declining income and property taxes, these revenue gains, however, proved inadequate.

In the midst of unrealistic revenue estimates, Bing resorted to the municipality's habit of borrowing to cover expenses. To buy time to tighten the city's operations and squeeze payroll costs, in November

2009 Detroit borrowed some $94 million in one-year tax anticipation notes to meet the continued revenue shortfall.[8] Then, in 2010, the city obtained $250 million by issuing fiscal stabilization bonds, backed by future state revenue-sharing payments.[9] However, borrowing money could not get Detroit out of its fiscal crisis.

On the critical expenditure side, Bing, with the city council's help, reduced expenses. During Bing's first three years in office (2009 to mid-2012), the city decreased its workforce from some 13,400 to about 10,000 employees. In 2009, he imposed a 10 percent wage cut through twenty-six unpaid furlough days on the city's nonunionized executive and legislative branch and local court employees. In October 2010, Bing, with the city council's agreement, instituted a 10 percent pay cut, again through twenty-six unpaid furlough days, and implemented certain health insurance concessions, among other cost savings, on virtually all other city employees, except for police officers and firefighters.[10]

The 2010 and 2011 Budget Battles

During Mayor Bing's first two years in office, Detroit faced an ongoing difficulty in balancing its revenues and expenditures that resulted in a continued structural budget deficit. At the same time, Bing experienced a rocky, if not tumultuous, relationship with the city council's realistic reform wing, which favored a more aggressive response to Detroit's financial condition.

Believing that government has a core responsibility to help people by providing services and meeting constituents' needs,[11] Bing tangled with the city council in 2010 and 2011, when council members called for even deeper budget cuts than he wanted to make. The council voted to override the mayor's budget in both years before reaching compromises—with Bing threatening service shutdowns each time, if the council did not restore funds to the budget. However, engaging in petty politicking, both the city council and the mayor fought over millions of dollars, even tens of millions of dollars, not the hundreds of millions of dollars required to prevent insolvency and restore fiscal sanity to Detroit. City leaders could not face the scale of Detroit's financial problems.

In 2010, the council gave in and restored $17.8 million to Bing's 2010–11 proposed budget that had already cut $100 million from the city's general fund by trimming spending in most departments by 4 to 16 percent. Instead of an additional $31.8 million in cuts as proposed by the council, the deal restored: (1) $4.6 million of the $6.7 million the council cut from the Police Department's budget, which would have resulted in laying off some one hundred police officers; (2) $1.8 million of the $3 million proposed trimming from the Fire Department's budget; (3) $5.5 million of $9.2 million the council cut from the General Services Department's funds for park maintenance and grass mowing, thereby saving seventy-seven city parks from closing; (4) some $2.6 million in funds to preserve the jobs of 33 out of 180 emergency medical service workers.[12]

Bing engaged in another budget battle with the city council in 2011. Although Bing and the council seemed at a budget impasse, the showdown resulted in a compromise that avoided devastating public services, at least temporarily. For the 2011–12 fiscal year, Bing's proposed budget had already reduced expenses by $200 million through, among other cuts, suspending for one year the $65 million annual loss recovery payment to the public employees' pension system. Believing that the mayor's revenue projections were too optimistic—especially with respect to the property tax revenues, and that he relied on economic growth that might not happen for some time—in May 2011 the council cut an extra $50 million from Bing's proposed budget. Then, in June 2011 Bing and the council reached a compromise on the budgetary cuts. The council reinstated $25 million to the city's spending plan.[13] The compromise restored $18.9 million in public safety funds, salvaging hundreds of police and firefighter jobs, as well as maintaining Sunday and twenty-four-hour bus service and keeping recreation centers open. The 2011 deal reinstituted: (1) $6.3 million out of $8.3 million of proposed cuts from the Police Department that would have resulted in fewer homicide investigations and police patrolling the streets; (2) $3.0 million of $4.1 million targeted to be slashed from the Fire Department, otherwise more than one hundred firefighters would have lost their jobs; (3) $7.4 million of $7.8 million in proposed reductions from the Detroit Department of Transportation that would have ended Sunday, holiday, and twenty-four-hour bus service, with bus riders having to face longer waits Monday through Saturday; (4) $2.2 million of $3.2 million in cuts put forward to the Recreation Department that would have closed certain public swimming pools and two recreation centers, left park grass uncut, and closed the downtown Hart Plaza to popular events. Although the deal still left Bing with the task of eliminating $4.7 million from the budget, the cuts did not go far enough. Whereas some council members pressed for across-the-board expenditure reductions and massive layoffs, the mayor banked on concessions from municipal employee unions. However, Bing's actions did not accompany his tough talk and his hollow threats to the city's labor unions. Presumably, he did not want to offend a key constituency in his bid for a second term.

Sliding into Insolvency

From July 2011 until the conclusion of the city–state April 2012 deal, the possible appointment of an unelected emergency manager hung over Detroit. Under legislation championed by Governor Richard D. (Rick) Snyder (R) and enacted in March 2011—but suspended in August 2012 and repealed in November of that year—the state obtained even broader authority than previously to appoint an emergency manager to take over many of the powers of local officials.[14] To reduce a city's budgetary deficit, for example, an emergency manager could abrogate or modify existing union contracts to decrease municipal employees' salaries and benefits and change work rules.

In the spring of 2011, an arbitration ruling went in Bing's favor. Hope existed that he could reduce all municipal employees' wages and benefits, thereby saving Detroit from fiscal disaster.

In April 2011, the city won an arbitration ruling with respect to the higher ranking police officers' benefits.[15] As a result of the ruling, Detroit police lieutenants and sergeants would see: (1) a cut in the rate at which these higher ranking officers would earn pension benefits by lowering the multiplier used to calculate the retirement pay in their existing defined benefit plan from 2.5 to 2.1 percent for benefits earned after September 1, 2011; (2) the elimination of cost-of-living increases on pensions earned after that date; (3) a suspension for two years in their longevity pay. The ruling also created a defined contribution plan for bargaining unit members who entered the Police Department after July 1, 2012.

Largely mirroring the arbitration ruling, the city obtained an agreement, effective after September 30, 2011, with unions representing Detroit's police officers. The one-year deal froze wages; reduced the multiplier used to calculate pensions from 2.5 to 2.1 percent, thereby slowing the rate at which police officers currently on the payroll would accrue pension benefits; and eliminated cost-of-living pension increases.[16] New hires brought into the department would participate in a defined contribution plan and contribute 10 percent of their salary to this plan. A subsequent February 2012 agreement between the city and the police officers' unions froze wages through 2015, increased health care insurance co-payments by union members, and restricted overtime, among other givebacks.[17]

In the second half of 2011 and the first quarter of 2012, Bing continued to seek wage and benefit concessions from other municipal employee unions. Whether the mayor botched the bargaining with the unions or they dug in, the unions balked at making substantial concessions. By March 2012, a group of some thirty unions ratified tentative agreements, subject to city council approval, continuing the pay freeze based on an extension of the previous 10 percent pay cut, accepting minor changes in health care benefits (but not an increase in employee payments for health-insurance costs), and placing new employees into defined contribution retirement plans.[18]

As the city faced entering into an agreement with the state, the appointment of an emergency manager, or bankruptcy, in early 2012 negotiations between the city officials and the governor grew more acrimonious. Political brinksmanship between the city and the state rapidly mounted. City residents expressed strident opposition to state control through the appointment of an emergency manager. The takeover of a black city with a black mayor and city council by an unelected emergency manager appointed by a white governor became racially charged. Focusing on a loss of local control even under a city–state deal, some council members resented the implication that they were not up to the task; others saw it as a union-busting move. Although wanting to work with the city and strike a deal, Governor Snyder viewed the tentative union agreements negotiated by Mayor Bing as inadequate because they failed to reduce expenses sufficiently.[19] The governor wanted more savings and revised work rules that otherwise prevented employees from being trained to do work outside certain job categories.

Hope for Fiscal Sanity

By the fall of 2011, realistic city and state leaders saw that Detroit was on a path to financial disaster.[20] It took a two-step process—first, the report of a state-appointed Financial Review Team, and second, the negotiation of a consent agreement—to begin Detroit's financial turnaround.

In January 2012, the ten-member state-appointed Financial Review Team began examining the city's financial plight. By late March, the team unanimously agreed that Detroit suffered from "severe financial stress."[21] The team concluded that Detroit's financial problems had grown over the years from many sources, including unrealistic revenue estimates in the context of a declining tax base; an inability to match expenditures with shrinking revenues, with the city annually spending some $150 million in excess of cash received; and repeatedly borrowing to cover budgetary deficits and finance its operations.

With the city's cash nearly running out and facing a cash-flow crisis—with a negative cash balance of some $44 million projected by the end of June 2012—the governor and the mayor fashioned a collaborative financial arrangement, the Financial Stability Agreement.[22] The council reluctantly approved the agreement by the slimmest of margins, 5 to 4, thereby avoiding the appointment of an emergency manager or bankruptcy, at least in 2012.

Three major legal challenges to the Financial Review Team's authority and the execution and implementation of the agreement were beaten back. A Michigan appellate court cleared the way for Governor Snyder, the state treasurer, and the Financial Review Team to negotiate and sign the agreement with the city, reversing an earlier trial court decision that barred the state from entering into the arrangement. The Michigan Supreme Court declined to intervene in the dispute.[23] A federal judge also denied a request from Detroit's largest employee union, the American Federation of State County and Municipal Employees Council 25, to block the governor and state treasurer from executing the agreement.[24] Finally, a state trial court dismissed an unauthorized, spurious lawsuit filed by Detroit's Corporation Counsel to block the implementation of the agreement.[25]

In the short term, the arrangement cleared the way for the state to help solve the city's immediate cash crunch.[26] The city entered into a financing arrangement that provided $137 million, initially $76 million by the end of March 2012, in financing through the private placement of anticipation bonds secured by liens on state revenue-sharing funds. This financing enabled the city to meet employee salaries and pay vendors. A subsequent August 2012 refinancing consisting of revenue bonds, again secured by the city's state revenue-sharing money, in part, paid off the March interim borrowing.

An Overview of the Financial Stability Agreement

In reaching the deal to avoid a 2012 takeover by a state-appointed emergency manager, the state and the city agreed to share financial power in a bid to keep Detroit solvent. The mayor and the city council remained in office—albeit with reduced powers and the need to live within the city's financial means, by controlling spending and paying down its accumulated deficit.

The Financial Stability Agreement created a nine-member Financial Advisory Board (FAB) to oversee the city's fiscal restructuring, in a declining revenue environment. Prior to the appointment of an emergency manager in March 2013, the FAB was composed of nine members: three appointed by the governor, two by the mayor, two by the city council, one by the state treasurer, and one appointed jointly by the mayor and the governor, subject to council approval, with the city and state splitting the board's cost. The board had the power to review, monitor, and advise the city on its budget, debt issuance, municipal reorganization, management practices, and general financial matters. It monitored Detroit's financial and operational performance. As part of the arrangement, the city had to establish a three-year, rolling planning budget, with expenses not in excess of income, designed to eliminate any current or accumulated deficit within five years.[27]

In light of prior budgets city officials adopted that "knowingly over-estimated revenues,"[28] the board had to approve the revenue estimate that formed the basis of the mayor's proposed annual budget and the council's subsequent budgetary approval. The revenue estimate had to be based on realistic, independent projections. The mayor agreed not to propose and the council agreed not to approve a budget with revenue projections different from the FAB- or state treasurer-approved revenue estimate. The mayor and council further agreed to reduce spending in any fiscal year if the budget went out of balance.

The agreement created two new city-paid executives, a Chief Financial Officer (CFO), which Detroit previously did not have, and a Program Management Director (PMD). The CFO supervised all of the city's financial and budgetary activities. The PMD, as head of the new Program Management Office, supervised the carrying out of a Financial Reform Plan (FRP). Based on a twenty-point list of projects in the city's Operational Reform Program, the FRP included changes in various departments, among them public lighting, transportation, health and wellness, and human services, as well as health care and pension modifications. The agreement also allowed for the outsourcing or privatization of some services as well as departmental consolidations.

An Attempted Path to Fiscal Sanity and Sustainability

Under the Financial Stability Agreement, Detroit had to pursue municipal fiscal discipline, in theory, no matter how painful for its employees and retirees, by bringing expenses into balance with declining revenues. Detroit's income tax receipts plummeted from about $277 million in fiscal year 2007–08 to about $221 million in fiscal year 2011–12. Revenues from real property taxes dropped by 20 percent from fiscal year 2007–08 to fiscal year 2011–12, from about $254 million to under $200 million, and now account for only 12 to 14 percent of the city's general receipts.[29]

In shaping the 2012–13 budget,[30] the first crafted with state oversight of the city's finances, the mayor and the council initially worked harmoniously, trimming the city's general fund expenditures by some $246 million, with $170 million in spending reductions and $76 million allocated to paying down the city's accumulated deficit. Cuts included a projected 10 percent pay reduction for all city workers, but eliminated furlough days and increased health care cost-sharing by employees to 20 percent along with higher co-pays and deductibles. The budget decreased the city's workforce by some 2,300 (2,254) people from every department, or more than 20 percent of its employees, starting July 1, 2012, mostly through layoffs but also as a result of retirements and attrition.

Public safety faced the axe. The budget slashed the Police Department's budget by some $90 million (or more than 13 percent) to $340 million.[31] It cut the Fire Department's budget by 13 percent from $183 million to $160 million,[32] to handle not only fire suppression and prevention but also emergency medical services to provide pre-hospital care and transportation for the sick and injured.[33] A Federal SAFER (Staffing for Adequate Fire and Emergency Response) program grant of $22.5 million saved 108 firefighter jobs for two years out of 164 threatened with layoffs.[34]

With respect to the Recreation Department, the budget reduced the appropriation from about $18 million to $12.3 million.[35] The reduction in funds was restored through the mayor's efforts. A new nonprofit organization, the Detroit Recreation Trust, will receive some $15 million from private and other public sources, including $5 million over a ten-year period from the Lear Corp., $2 million from The General Motors Foundation, and $3 million in federal Community Development Block Grant funds, to keep the city's recreation centers open.[36] The municipal funds budgeted for recreation centers will be used mainly for the upkeep of buildings needed to stay open to help stabilize neighborhoods.

Changes occurred in three other departments, Health and Wellness Promotion, Workforce Development, and Human Services. With the budget only providing the Department of Health and Wellness

Promotion with six months' additional funding,[37] effective October 1, 2012, the department's functions were transferred to the Institute for Population Health (IPH). The IPH will be run with the federal dollars the city receives. The budget eliminated the Detroit Workforce Development Department[38] with its functions transferred to Detroit Employment Solutions, a nonprofit organization governed by an eleven-member board of directors appointed by the mayor. Although funded for a full year,[39] the budget outsourced the functions of the Human Services Department to charitable and social services organizations.

Cultural organizations saw their subsidies cut. For example, the general fund's subsidy for the Detroit Institute of Arts went from $375,000 to zero.

The Showdown over Public Employee Pay and Benefit Cuts

With respect to the all-important labor provisions, the Financial Stability Agreement sought to impose tough terms regarding wages, benefits, and work rules in new union contracts. Under the agreement, the mayor consented not to propose or sign and the council concurred not to endorse any union agreements containing provisions not approved by the state treasurer. If the council failed to approve a union contract as proposed by the mayor and approved by the FAB, the Program Management Director could approve the agreement.

In July 2012, over the objections of municipal employee union leaders and a majority (5 to 4) of council members, Detroit cut the pay and strengthened the work rules for many of its unionized workers. The cutbacks and additional layoffs were aimed at saving some $102 million a year, otherwise the city would have run out of cash as early as October 2012. Although painful to employees and their families, doing something allowed Detroit to fix its severe financial troubles, at least in the short term, in an orderly manner.

The Financial Stability Agreement permitted new contracts to impose terms, such as pay and benefit cuts, without union approval. Under the agreement, the city was exempt as of July 16, 2012, from its obligation to bargain collectively under the Michigan Public Employment Relations Act.[40]

Facing municipal insolvency, Mayor Bing at last found his backbone. After union contracts with most of the city's workers expired at the end of June, Bing imposed 10 percent wage cuts for members of the city's unions, including police officers and firefighters.[41] In addition, city employees faced pension reductions; health-care changes, particularly increased out-of-pocket costs; a variety of work-rule changes designed to enhance flexibility and produce financial savings; and an end to supplemental unemployment benefits beyond legal requirements.[42] The city council, by a largely symbolic 5 to 4 vote, declined to go along with the 2012 wage and benefit cuts and other changes. However, the mayor, the Financial Advisory Board, and the city's Program Management Director signed off, thereby imposing the terms on union members.

For those unionized city employees subject to contracts that did not expire in 2012, the emergency manager will be able to impose these changes in 2013. The contractual changes imposed in 2012 do not, however, affect unionized workers, such as those with the Department of Transportation, whose units receive federal funds.

A Preliminary Assessment of the Financial Stability Agreement

The Financial Stability Agreement failed to enable Detroit to overcome its fiscal challenges. The appointments of the four FAB members by the city and the state and the one hybrid appointment made it difficult to make hard decisions in the face of entrenched union opposition and residents' resistance to massive service cutbacks. But given the FAB's role to review, monitor, and advise, subject to its power to approve revenue estimates and any debt issuance, the board lacked sufficient powers.

Detroit's cash position remains precarious, rendering bankruptcy a possibility, even with the appointment of an emergency manager. Continued cash-flow difficulties and a projected deficit in excess of $100 million at the end of its 2013 fiscal year make noncritical public service furloughs and more layoffs inevitable. Increased employee contributions to health care plans are also likely.

The Possibilities for Outsourcing Services and Privatizing Assets

Going forward, Detroit's officials must carefully analyze what activities to give over to other providers that will perform these better at a lower cost. Consideration must also be given to the sale of city-owned assets.

Outsourcing Functions. Possibilities for outsourcing services to the private sector include the functions performed by the Department of Public Works, the General Services Department, and the Department of Transportation. In addition to serving as the lead agency for inspection and blight enforcement throughout the city, the Solid Waste Division of the Department of Public Works supplies the following collection services: weekly refuse for residential households; quarterly curbside bulk; seasonal yard waste as well as the curbside recycling program in designated areas. With respect to garbage collection, Detroit could outsource this service by contracting with a private firm to furnish this function. Outsourcing could save the city upwards of 30 percent from its annual total refuse bill.[43] Even the threat of outsourcing would likely force city employees to provide better service for less money. The department also supplies street-related services, such as road repairs and resurfacing, as well as major street sweeping and snow removal. These functions could be turned over to private firms.

The General Services Department has four divisions, three of which offer outsourcing possibilities, as well as one unit of a division. Its Grounds Maintenance and Forestry Division maintains city-owned grounds, parks, and vacant lots, including cutting grass and removing litter at major city parks, and manages snow and ice removal at municipal facilities. Its Fleet Management Division procures, maintains, and makes available the city's 3,100 vehicles. Its Facilities Planning and Management Division manages city-owned properties, including space planning, building operations and maintenance, and engineering work. This division's Building Services unit handles janitorial services at city-owned facilities.

Bus service in Detroit, provided by the Department of Transportation, has long lacked dependability and reliability. The city system, which does not interface with the suburban system, struggles to maintain schedules and keep its fleet service-ready. Riders, who depend on buses for access to employment, government offices, health care, and education, often wait hours for overcrowded buses that break down too often.[44]

Finally, the city undertook restructuring its bus service. In February 2012, it brought in a private contractor to manage the system.[45] Thereafter, various adjustments—including eliminating 1:00 AM–4:00 AM bus service, cutting some routes, lengthening the wait times on dozens of lines, and increasing service on four of its busiest lines—were made.[46] Through these route rationalizations, the private contractor hopes to improve on-time performance and achieve cost savings.[47]

After these restructurings bring bus service to an acceptable level, the 2012–13 budget proposed outsourcing the operation to a third party.[48] The city would transfer the functions of the Department of Transportation, which has responsibility for the city's bus routes, to a private third-party vendor that would manage the operations and overall administration. In the meantime, the 2012–13 budget held the city's bus transit subsidy at about $53 million, with only a $100,000 decrease from fiscal year 2011–12.

It is unclear what entity would enter into the bus takeover with the city and on what terms. Possible arrangements include competitive franchising, where the city could franchise the entire bus system to one firm for a period of up to twenty years, or competitive contracting, where the city could competitively bid out all of its bus services to a number of firms through separate contracts that would be rebid at least every five years. In either case, by contract the city would maintain its right to establish routes, fares, and service standards.[49] In addition to providing better service, one or more contractors would pay taxes to the city, thereby enhancing municipal revenues.

Selling Assets. To raise funds and help reduce expenses, the city could look to sell certain of its publicly owned assets. Possibilities include the municipal airport, its lighting system, the Detroit Public Lighting Department, and possibly its parking system. The 2012–13 budget sought to transfer the city airport, the Coleman A. Young International Airport, which needs capital improvements to make it a twenty-first century facility, to either a new independent public airport authority; the Wayne County Airport Authority; the State of Michigan Department of Transportation–Aeronautics Division; or some type of joint venture, perhaps a public-private partnership. The budget provided six months of funding for the airport, to give the city time to find a viable alternative. However, the airport likely has limited appeal to others, given that the facility is land-locked, thus constricting future expansion opportunities, and has limited current runway capacity.

The 2012–13 budget also proposed the partial privatization of the Department of Public Lighting (DPL). The DPL maintains and operates the city's street lights and traffic signals as well as an electricity grid system. With its aging, inefficient facilities, the out-of-date system poses a source of aggravation for residents and renders neighborhoods unsafe. Street lights do not work from night to night. Traffic signals, powered by the DPL, constantly fail. Antiquated equipment, after years of neglect, characterizes the DPL's poor condition and its unreliable service. The electricity grid faces revenue collection problems and a lack of economies of scale given its relatively small operation.

Since 1884, the city has engaged in supplying electricity. Currently, Detroit provides a subsidy of some $9 ($9.44) million a year to the DPL to cover its shortfall in expected revenues. In addition to maintaining the city's street lights and traffic signal system, the department supplies power to some public buildings in the city as well as to 35,000 out of 88,000 street lights, with DTE Energy supplying electricity to the remaining street lights.

Power outages are pervasive.[50] In 2000, Detroit suffered its worst blackout in history. The four-day incident knocked out electricity to about 4,500 buildings, including police precincts, fire stations, libraries, and Detroit Receiving Hospital. Most street and traffic lights lost power. Again in 2001, the city suffered another partial power outage. In June 2011, a twenty-four-hour power failure cut off electricity to the courts, city hall, Wayne State University, the Cobo Center, ten Detroit public schools, the Detroit People Mover (a largely empty, fully automated light rail system operating on an elevated, single track, 2.9-mile loop in Detroit's central business district), the Detroit Institute of Arts, and the Detroit Historical Museum.

Today, the city lacks the funds to modernize its street light operations and the electricity grid, which are more than one hundred years old. The system needs a huge capital investment of $140 million to $200 million to update the street lighting system, and a $100-million upgrade for electricity transmission and distribution. Additionally, at least $5 million is needed annually to cover the cost of operations.[51]

The 2012–13 budget contained a long-term plan to transfer street lighting operations to an independent public lighting authority having the ability to issue debt.[52] The transfer became a reality with the enactment of state legislation creating the Municipal Lighting Authority—enabling the use of a utility users' tax to annually pay interest and principal on bonds to finance $160 million in capital improvements, and suspending the city's income tax rollback as an additional revenue source.

The new authority will reduce the number of street and alley lights to under 50,000 (46,000), including every light in city alleys, two-thirds of the lights in declining neighborhoods, and one-third of the lights in more stable neighborhoods. The new lighting system will cater to Detroit's current population centers, hopefully providing reliable service and added safety where most needed, such as at schools and intersections. Besides the immediate repair of lights on major thoroughfares, the four-year overhaul project, as proposed, will take place in phases, seemingly with the top tier neighborhoods receiving priority.[53]

The budget also calls for the transfer of the electricity grid over a seven-year period to a third-party operator, again presumably DTE

Energy, thereby ensuring a more reliable power supply to Detroit. The transition would involve moving the system's existing customers to third-party-owned meters and beginning to transfer the electrical grid and power lines on a substation by substation basis, ultimately selling the thirty substations the DPL owns.[54] In addition to providing better service, privatization of the electricity grid would generate a one-time influx of cash. In private hands, the system would generate property and corporate taxes for the city.

At present, it is unclear what entity would want to take over DPL's power function, on what terms, and with what impact on rates. Also, would a private party undertake the needed capital improvements?[55]

The Search for Revenues

To raise funds to meet its expenses the city must enhance its revenues and rebuild its tax base. These efforts could include better collection of various taxes and fines, such as real property and income taxes as well as blight fines. Specific possibilities include identifying suburban employers who fail to withhold city income tax from Detroit residents they employ, and partnering with the Internal Revenue Service to identify those not paying city taxes, including non-filers and cheats. The city must also gather more funds owed by insurance companies and uninsured patients for ambulance runs,[56] and step up the collection of parking violation fines. The garnering of taxes, fines, and fees could be outsourced to the Wayne County Treasurer or a private for-profit firm.

Detroit must rebuild its tax base by attracting new firms and residents. New businesses, including large corporations, start-ups, and firms from overseas, will boost municipal revenues. Conversely, the city must avoid the imposition of any new (or increased) taxes on businesses and residents. Someday Detroit officials will realize that people and employers are mobile. High (and ever higher) taxes will discourage in-migration and encourage out-migration.

The Need for Debt Reduction

In addition to balancing its budget and eliminating its accumulated deficit, Detroit must generate surpluses to begin to pay down its huge debt.[57] The city's long-term liabilities, including unfunded pension liabilities for its various employee systems and its health care obligations, equal about $15 billion, depending on whether certain pension system assets are added in. To meet part of its unfunded pension obligations, in 2005 and 2006 the city issued Pension Funding Certificates. The service payments on these certificates will equal about $120 million a year through mid-2035. Independent actuaries now have concluded that Detroit's pension funds remain significantly underfunded and its health care liabilities may be higher than previously estimated.[58] Furthermore, the ratio of the city's long-term debt to its total net assets equaled an astounding 32.64 to 1 in 2010. During Bing's tenure, the three major credit rating agencies repeatedly downgraded the city's general obligation debt to ever-lower rungs of junk (speculative or highly speculative, non-investment) status, triggering the violation of interest rate swap contracts, unless renegotiated, that could force the impoverished city to pay millions of dollars to counter-party banks.[59]

Detroiters face decades of austerity to fund pension and other post-employment obligations and pay down some $8.6 billion in long-term debt. At least a generation will pay for the past generation's profligacy and the overreaching of city employee unions.

Without bankruptcy relief, reforming pensions and cutting health care costs assume paramount importance, despite union opposition. Detroit pays pension and health care benefits far larger than it can afford. As is true of many states, counties, and municipalities, Detroit's pension and health care costs are enormous and crushing. Employee benefit expenses make up one-half of the city's annual general fund expenditures. In particular, the city's various outlays on pensions equal about $295 million annually. Another $285 million a year go for its employees' and retirees' health care costs.[60]

Simply put, city employees must pay more toward their pensions and health care. This will likely be possible with the appointment of an emergency manager. Besides putting future employees into defined contribution plans, retirement benefits must be cut for current and newly hired workers. Although the Michigan Constitution protects accrued benefits in defined benefits plans,[61] consideration must be given to freezing these benefits for current employees, getting existing workers into defined contribution arrangements, and raising the retirement age. In other states, taking the lead, voters have approved pension cuts for municipal employees.[62] In addition to eliminating dental and vision coverage for retirees in 2013, increasing retiree contributions to their health care costs must be considered.

After tackling its pension and health care costs, Detroit must prioritize its public services, concentrate its limited resources on key activities, and limit the city from providing things it cannot afford or do efficiently. In addition to identifying core undertakings, each municipal department must justify its existence. The functions performed by each and every city employee must be scrutinized. Union feather-bedding must go; work rules must be further revised. Careful analysis must ask: Is each worker needed? Can one employee do the work of several current jobholders? The city must also effectively use technology in managing its employees' deployment.

It is probable that Detroit will overcome years of fiscal mismanagement and achieve financial stability and sustainability. However, even with the appointment of an emergency manager, bankruptcy remains a possibility, particularly if the city cannot bring its expenses in line with its revenues.

At the same time as Detroit officials worked to secure its fiscal survival, the city, led by Mayor Bing, sought to rightsize the municipal government by reducing services and encouraging residents to cluster in its healthiest neighborhoods—those with high-quality housing stock as well as close proximity to schools, other public services, and amenities. We turn and consider Bing's plans—which proved controversial and were ultimately watered down—to redistribute population to match available public services.

Notes

1. For background on Mayor Bing, see Michael Rosenberg, "Having Fun Yet, Mr. Mayor?," *Sports Illustrated* 112:2 (January 18, 2010): 66–72; Stephen Moore, "The Weekend Interview with Dave Bing: Can Detroit Be Saved?," *Wall Street Journal*, December 19, 2009, A11.

2. Darren A. Nichols, David Josar, Leonard N. Fleming, "New council vows Detroit 'revolution,'" *Detroit News*, November 5, 2009, A1.

3. State of Michigan, Department of Treasury, Report of the Detroit Financial Review Team (Report of the Detroit Financial Review Team), March 26, 2012, 3, 4.

4. Leonard N. Fleming, "Ex-aides: Bing's office a battle of personalities," *Detroit News*, June 2, 2011, A1. See also Leonard N. Fleming, "Detroit deputy mayor resigns," *Detroit News*, May 24, 2011, A1, and Daniel Howes, "Bing drags feet on fixing Detroit," *Detroit News*, May 27, 2011, A10.

5. Leonard N. Fleming, "Lewis brings stability back to Bing administration," *Detroit News*, August 29, 2011, A1, and Tom Walsh, "Bing, Lewis mend fences," *Detroit Free Press*, July 29, 2011, A12.

6. City of Detroit, Discussion Document, July 16, 2012, 27 (Appendix 3) and Standard & Poor's, Detroit, Michigan; Appropriations; General Obligation, General Credit Portal, Ratings Direct, June 28, 2011, 2 <www.standardandpoors.com/ratingsdirect>.

7. Report of Detroit Financial Review Team, 6.
8. Memo from Irvin Corley, Jr., Director, Detroit City Council, Fiscal Analysis Division to Detroit City Council Members, October 13, 2009.
9. Report of Detroit Financial Review Team, 6.
10. Darren A. Nichols, "Council lowers AFSCME pay 10%," *Detroit News*, September 29, 2010, A3, and Steve Neavling, "Union," *Detroit Free Press*, September 29, 2010, A3. See also Suzette Hackney, "Survival at heart of stalemate," *Detroit Free Press*, August 31, 2010, A2.
11. Moore, "Interview."
12. For the saga of the 2010 budget battle, see Christine MacDonald and Darren A. Nichols, "Tensions high in wake of budget shutdown," *Detroit News*, June 30, 2010, A3; Naomi R. Patton and Suzette Hackney, "Council rescues Detroit's parks," *Detroit Free Press*, June 30, 2010, A3; Christine Mac-Donald and Darren A. Nichols, "Mayor, council reach budget deal," *Detroit News*, June 29, 2010, A1; Christine MacDonald and Darren A. Nichols, "Detroit City Council's budget plan would keep parks open," *Detroit News*, June 26, 2010, A3; Suzette Hackney and Naomi R. Patton, "Bing details plans to slash city budget," *Detroit Free Press*, June 11, 2010, A4; Darren A. Nichols, "Council reverses veto on budget," *Detroit News*, June 5, 2010, A3; Suzette Hackney, "Bing: Layoffs for police, firefighters next," *Detroit Free Press*, June 9, 2010, A15; Naomi R. Patton, "Bing threatening more cuts," *Detroit Free Press*, June 5, 2010, A3; Suzette Hackney and Naomi R. Patton, "Detroit Mayor vetoes budget," *Detroit Free Press*, June 3, 2010, A6; Darren A. Nichols and Leonard N. Fleming, "Bing vetoes council's budget plan," *Detroit News*, June 3, 2010, A4; Darren A. Nichols, "Council trims Bing's budget," *Detroit News*, May 22, 2010, A5; Naomi R. Patton, "Council trims Bing's budget," *Detroit News*, May 22, 2010, A5; Suzette Hackney, "Bing tries to make good on his budget promises," *Detroit Free Press*, April 14, 2010, A4; Leonard N. Fleming and Darren A. Nichols, "Bing says it's 'now or never' to fix budget," *Detroit News*, April 14, 2010, A1; Leonard N. Fleming, "Bing, council squabble as budget talks near," *Detroit News*, April 12, 2010, A1. See also City of Detroit, Office of the Auditor General, Analysis of the Mayor's 2010-2011 Proposed Budget, April 30, 2010.
13. City of Detroit, Office of the Auditor General, Analysis of the Mayor's 2011–2012 Proposed Budget, n.d., and The Detroit City Council 2011-2012 Financial and Budgetary Priorities, Public Policy, Planning and Action Resolution, May 24, 2011.
   For the tale of the 2011 budget battle, see Darren A. Nichols, "Job, service cuts cloud dawn of Detroit fiscal year," *Detroit News*, July 2, 2011, A3; Steve Neavling and Elisha Anderson, "Detroit cuts won't be as deep feared," *Detroit Free Press*, July 1, 2011, A1; Darren A. Nichols, "Bing, council split the difference," *Detroit News*, July 1, 2011, A1; Darren A. Nichols, "Bing offers budget compromise," *Detroit News*, June 30, 2011, A1; Steve Neavling, "Bing back with new budget proposal," *Detroit Free Press*, June 30, 2011, A1; Steve Neavling, Katelyn Abdilla, Aaron Snyder, "Detroit's budget standoff," *Detroit Free Press*, June 29, 2011, A1; Darren A. Nichols and Leonard N. Fleming, "No budget deal," *Detroit News*, June 29, 2011, A1; Steve Neavling, "Budget-deal vote expected today," *Detroit Free Press*, June 28, 2011, A4; Steve Neavling, "Cuts still sore point for Detroit council," *Detroit Free Press*,

June 23, 2011, A4; Steve Neavling, "City Council, Mayor in budget impasse," *Detroit Free Press*, June 22, 2011, A4; Steve Neavling, "Bing: Hart Plaza festivals in peril," *Detroit Free Press*, June 14, 2011, A1; Darren A. Nichols, "Council balks at Bing bid to restore $30M in cuts," *Detroit News*, June 15, 2011, A4; Darren A. Nichols, "Bing says budget cuts to hit parks and transit," *Detroit News*, June 14, 2011, A1; Steve Neavling, "Council restores $50M in cuts," *Detroit Free Press*, June 7, 2011, A1; Steve Neavling, "Detroit council to override Bing on $50M in cuts to city budget," *Detroit Free Press*, June 2, 2011, A4; Suzette Hackney, "Bing, council spar over police cuts," *Detroit Free Press*, May 25, 2011, A1; Darren A. Nichols, "Bing, council at odds over public safety reductions," *Detroit News*, May 25, 2011; A1; Darren A. Nichols, "Bing, council spar over budget cuts," *Detroit News*, May 24, 2011, A4; Darren A. Nichols, "Council seeks police, arts cuts," *Detroit News*, May 19, 2011, A1; Steve Neavling, "Council balks at Bing's plan for city deficit," *Detroit Free Press*, May 7, 2011, A3; Darren A. Nichols, "Plan to cut deficit unveiled," *Detroit News*, May 5, 2011, A4; Darren A. Nichols and Leonard N. Fleming," Bing plan retains jobs, cuts spending," *Detroit News*, April 13, 2011, A1; Suzette Hackney and Matt Helms, "Detroit budget full of tough calls, tough cuts," *Detroit Free Press*, April 13, 2011, A1.

14. Michigan Public Act 4 of 2011 (the Local Government and School District Fiscal Accountability Act), Michigan Compiled Laws Annotated Section 141.1501. The act was suspended in August 2012, repealed by voters in November 2012, and replaced by the Local Financial Stability and Choice Act enacted in December 2012. For a summary of the 2011 act see City of Detroit, Office of the Auditor General, Analysis of the Mayor's 2011–2012 Proposed Budget, Appendix A, x–xvii. See also State of Michigan, Department of Treasury, Frequently Asked Questions Regarding Public Act 4 of 2011, the Local Government and School District Fiscal Accountability Act, March 21, 2011 <www.michigan.gov/treasury>. For the prior legislation empowering the state to appoint emergency financial managers, see Public Act 72 of 1990 (the Local Government Fiscal Responsibility Act).

15. In the Matter of the City of Detroit v. Detroit Police Lieutenants and Sergeants Association, State of Michigan Compulsory Arbitration, Act 312 Arbitration Award, Case No. D09 G-0786, April 5, 2011. See also Leonard N. Fleming, "Pension ruling riles workers," *Detroit News*, April 27, 2011, A4.

16. Matthew Dolan, "Deal Slices Workers' Pensions in Detroit," *Wall Street Journal*, August 3, 2011, A3; Leonard N. Fleming, "Pension deal to save city millions," *Detroit News*, August 3, 2011, A1; Steve Neavling, "Detroit police OK changes to pension," *Detroit Free Press*, August 3, 2011, A3.

17. Leonard N. Fleming and Darren A. Nichols, "City, police reach concessions deal," *Detroit News*, February 11, 2011, A1, and Suzette Hackney and Gina Damron, "Bing gets tentative deal with cop unions," *Detroit Free Press*, February 11, 2011, A1.

18. Steve Neavling, "Detroit union concessions fall short of fixing crisis, state says," *Detroit Free Press*, March 24, 2012, A1; Steve Neavling and Suzette Hackney, "Union deal may not be enough to help city," *Detroit Free Press*, February 3, 2012, A1; Darren A. Nichols, "Detroit close to union deal," *Detroit News*, February 1, 2012, A4.

19. Suzette Hackney, "Bing says he was left with no choice on consent deal," *Detroit Free Press*, April 21, 2012, A1; Suzette Hackney, "Leaders approve a short-term fix," *Detroit Free Press*, March 28, 2012, A1; Suzette Hackney and Steve Neavling, "Detroit's in emergency, but a deal may be close," *Detroit Free Press*, March 27, 2012, A1; Suzette Hackney and Paul Egan, "City could learn its fate this week," *Detroit Free Press*, March 25, 2012, A8.

20. See, e.g., Detroit Mayor Dave Bing, Speech, "Financial Update," November 16, 2011 <http://www.detroitmi.gov/Departmentsand Agencies/Mayors Office/NewsRelease> (December 14, 2011). See also Monica Davey, "In TV Address, Mayor Urges Detroit to Accept Drastic Action to Fix Dire Finances," *New York Times*, November 17, 2011, A13; Matthew Dolan, "Mayor Makes Case for Cuts in Detroit," *Wall Street Journal*, November 17, 2011, A8; Suzette Hackney et al., "Bing: Saving city means sacrifice," *Detroit Free Press*, November 17, 2011, A1; Darren A. Nichols, Leonard N. Fleming, Karen Bouffard, "Bing makes call to action to fix city's fiscal crisis," *Detroit News*, November 17, 2011, A1; Daniel Howes, "It's now or never for Detroit to take control of its destiny," *Detroit News*, November 17, 2011, A1; Stephen Henderson, "Detroit's clock striking midnight," *Detroit Free Press*, November 16, 2011, A10; Darren A. Nichols and Leonard N. Fleming, "City's financial crisis comes to fore," *Detroit News*, November 16, 2011, A6.

21. Report of the Detroit Financial Review Team, 1, 11. See also Daniel Howes, "Detroit a financial wreck in report," *Detroit News*, March 29, 2012, A8; Steve Neavling, "Review team's report tells how city got into this mess," *Detroit Free Press*, March 28, 2012, A8; Steve Neavling, "Team: We will do what we must," *Detroit Free Press*, January 1, 2012, A1.

22. Financial Stability Agreement between the State of Michigan and the City of Detroit, April 10, 2012. Earlier draft versions include Financial Stability Agreement between the City of Detroit, the City of Detroit Financial Review Team, and the Treasurer for the State of Michigan, Draft of March 12, 2012. For the unfolding of the negotiations, see Hackney, "Bing says;" *Economist*, "Stalled in Motor City," 402:8779 (April 7, 2012): 40; Monica Davey, "For Detroit, a New Start on a Path to Recovery," *New York Times*, April 6, 2012, A11; Stephen Henderson, "City Council showed true leadership," *Detroit Free Press*, April 5, 2012, A1; Matt Helms and Kathleen Gray, "Detroit union leaders say workers are scapegoats in financial crisis," *Detroit Free Press*, April 5, 2012, A8; Leonard N. Fleming, Darren A. Nichols, Christine MacDonald, "Split council OKs consent deal," *Detroit News*, April 5, 2012, A1; Nolan Finley, "Difficult vote puts Detroit on right path," *Detroit News*, April 5, 2012, A1; Monica Davey, "Council Reluctantly Agrees to State's Oversight of Detroit's Fiscal Decisions," *New York Times*, April 5, 2012, A12; Matt Helms and Kathleen Gray, "Detroit's new deal," *Detroit Free Press*, April 5, 2012, A1; Steve Neavling, Matt Helms, David Ashenfelter, "Bing: Time to vote or Snyder will act," *Detroit Free Press*, April 4, 2012, A1; Leonard N. Fleming and Steve Pardo, "Consent agreement window shrinking," *Detroit News*, April 4, 2012, A1; Monica Davey, "Detroit, Staggering with Debt, Now Struggles with a Rescue Plan," *New York Times*, April 4, 2012, A10; Steve Neavling, Matt Helms, Dawson Bell, "Deal may be close but pitfalls loom," *Detroit Free Press*, April 3, 2012, A1; Paul Egan and Dawson Bell, "Detroit comes down to the wire," *Detroit Free Press*, April 2, 2012,

A1; Leonard N. Fleming, "EM takeover looms as City Council vote looms," *Detroit News*, April 2, 2012, A3; Christine MacDonald, "Detroit council may see consent deal as best option," March 31, 2012, A1; Chad Livengood and Karen Bouffard, "Consent plan calls for quasi EM," *Detroit News*, March 30, 2012, A7; Leonard N. Fleming and Steve Pardo, "Council slams state's latest rescue deal," March 30, 2012, A1; Suzette Hackney, "State pitches new plan," *Detroit Free Press*, March 30, 2012, A1; Christine MacDonald, Steve Pardo, Leonard N. Fleming, "New consent plan could impose labor contracts," *Detroit News*, March 30, 2012, A1; Suzette Hackney and Paul Egan, "State, city close in on financial agreement," *Detroit Free Press*, March 29, 2012, A9; Todd Spangler et al., "Fix our city," *Detroit Free Press*, March 29, 2012, A1; Leonard N. Fleming and Darren A. Nichols, "Council to review rescue plan today," *Detroit News*, March 29, 2012, A1; Nolan Finley, "Why Snyder may blink in Bing face-off," *Detroit News*, March 29, 2012, B2; Laura Berman, "Some Detroiters not convinced city needs emergency manager," *Detroit News*, March 29, 2012, A8; Hackney, "Leaders approve;" Steve Neavling, "6 on council met in private with the state," *Detroit Free Press*, March 28, 2012, A8; Darren A. Nichols and Leonard N. Fleming, "Detroit to borrow $137M to pay bills," *Detroit News*, March 28, 2012, A1; Leonard N. Fleming, Darren A. Nichols, Karen Bouffard, "Detroit, state inching closer to financial deal," *Detroit News*, March 27, 2012, A1; Hackney and Neavling, "Detroit's in emergency"; Nick Bunkley and Monica Davey, "Governor Sees Hope for a Deal with Detroit," *New York Times*, March 27, 2012, A1; Megha Satyanarayana et al., "Speaking up," *Detroit Free Press*, March 26, 2012, A1; Hackney and Egan, "City could learn its fate;" Darren A. Nichols, Karen Bouffard, Leonard N. Fleming, "Consent deal faces host of hurdles," *Detroit News*, March 23, 2012, A1; Paul Egan and Suzette Hackney, "A new hurdle for consent deal," *Detroit Free Press*, March 21, 2012, A1; Darren A. Nichols and David Shepardson, "Bing seeks state help to raise revenues for Detroit," *Detroit News*, March 20, 2012, A1; Matthew Dolan, "Detroit Struggles for a Fiscal Fix," *Wall Street Journal*, March 19, 2012, A2; Steve Neavling and Todd Spangler, "City's draft of deal would give Bing the power," *Detroit Free Press*, March 16, 2012, A1; Leonard N. Fleming, Darren A. Nichols, Karen Bouffard, "Ire over consent plan grows louder," *Detroit News*, March 15, 2012, A10; Suzette Hackney, Steve Neavling, Paul Egan, "Amid furor, city works on own plan," *Detroit Free Press*, March 15, 2012, A1; Darren A. Nichols and Leonard N. Fleming, "Bing: Snyder's consent plan 'will not solve our problems,'" *Detroit* News, March 14, 2012, A1; Suzette Hackney and Kathleen Gray, "Snyder's Detroit plan puts board in charge," *Detroit Free Press*, March 14, 2012, A1; Steve Yaccino, "Detroit Officials Criticize State's Proposal for Fiscal Oversight Panel," *New York Times*, March 14, 2012, A16; Corey Williams and Kathy Barks Hoffman, "State plan for Detroit finances would shift power," *Washington Post*, March 14, 2012, A2; Darren A. Nichols and Leonard N. Fleming, "Bing says state cash vital to turnaround, *Detroit News*, March 10, 2012, A3; Matthew Dolan, "Detroit's Mayor Asks Governor for Help," *Wall Street Journal*, March 9, 2012, A6; Monica Davey, "Mayor of Ailing Detroit Resists Outside Takeover," *New York Times*, March 8, 2012, A14; Leonard N. Fleming and Darren A. Nichols, "Bing asks state to help force concessions," *Detroit News*, March 8, 2012, A1; Krissah Thompson,

"Emergency manager plan draws criticism in Detroit," *Washington Post*, January 6, 2012, A3.

For a 2011-12 financial crisis timeline, see *Detroit Free Press*, "Key dates in the crisis," April 5, 2012, A9.

23. Davis v. City of Detroit Financial Review Team, 2012 Mich. App. LEXIS 987 (Mich. Ct. App. 2012), reversing Davis v. City of Detroit Financial Review Team, LC No. 12-000113-CZ (Mich. Circuit Ct. 2012) and McNeil v. City of Detroit Financial Review Team, LC No. 12-000321-CZ (Mich. Circuit Ct. 2012), appeal denied, 491 Mich. 907, 810 N.W. 2d 565 (2012). See also Paul Egan, "State's top court won't intervene in dispute," *Detroit Free Press*, April 21, 2012, A6, and Darren A. Nichols and Karen Bouffard, "Court clears path to consent deal," *Detroit News*, March 24, 2012, A1. See also Leonard N. Fleming, Steve Pardo, Christine MacDonald, "Ruling puts consent deal in limbo," *Detroit News*, April 3, 2012, A1.

24. Valenti v. Synder, 2012 U.S. Dist. LEXIS 47736 (E.D. Mich. April 4, 2012) and Valenti v. Snyder, 2012 U.S. Dist. LEXIS 49521 (E.D. Mich. April 4, 2012). See also Fleming, Nichols, MacDonald, "Split council."

25. Darren A. Nichols, Leonard N. Fleming, Karen Bouffard, "Detroit gets back to business," *Detroit News*, June 14, 2012, A1, and Paul Egan, Matt Helms, Suzette Hackney, "City moves on as judge squashes consent fight," *Detroit Free Press*, June 14, 2012, A1.

26. Reuters, "Bond sale to boost Detroit cash flow set for Thursday," August 10, 2012 <www.reuters.com/assets/print?aid=USLZE8JA88T2010810> (August 20, 2012) and City of Detroit, 2012-2013 Executive Budget Summary, A1.

27. In April 2011, Mayor Bing delivered a five-year Deficit Elimination Plan, requested by the city council, designed to reduce and then eliminate the city's accumulated deficit. The plan sought to restore the city's financial health by seeking to eliminate the causes of its structural budget deficit while providing residents with a meaningful quality of public services. City of Detroit, Deficit Elimination Plan, April 29, 2011.

28. Report of the Detroit Financial Review Team, 7.

29. City of Detroit, Office of the Auditor General, Analysis of the Mayor's 2012-2013 Proposed Budget (Budget Analysis), May 8, 2012, 5–8 (municipal income tax revenue), 9–11 (property tax revenue) and Citizens Research Council of Michigan, The Fiscal Condition of the City Of Detroit, Report 361, April 2010, 24–32. See also Mike Wilkinson, "Revenue falls faster than city's spending," *Detroit News*, April 19, 2012, A1. The impact of Ohio casinos, which opened beginning in May 2012, on Detroit's casino-related revenues is uncertain, but likely negative. Budget Analysis, 12–15 (casino-related revenue), 65, 66. See also John Gallagher and Matt Helms, "Ohio's casinos to cost Detroit," *Detroit Free Press*, May 13, 2012, A1, and Mike Wilkinson, "New Ohio gaming halls may cash in at Detroit's expense," *Detroit News*, May 5, 2012, A1.

30. City of Detroit, Budget Department, Adopted Budget for Fiscal 2012–2013 (2012–2013 Budget); City of Detroit, 2012-2013 Executive Budget Summary; Dave Bing (represented by Kirk Lewis), City of Detroit, Mayor's Budget Address FY 2012–2013, April 12, 2012. See also Darren A. Nichols, "Proposed city budget would cut 2,566 jobs," *Detroit News*, April 24, 2012, A1; Suzette Hackney and Matt Helms, "Bing's budget slashes 2,500 jobs, $250M," *Detroit*

Free Press, April 24, 2012, A1; Darren A. Nichols and Leonard N. Fleming, "Bing's budget would cut city spending by $160M," *Detroit News*, April 13, 2012, A1; Suzette Hackney and Matt Helms, "Public safety, transit among $160M in cuts," *Detroit Free Press*, April 13, 2012, A1.

Lewis became deputy mayor in March 2012, filling in for Bing during the mayor's illness. City of Detroit, Media Advisory, "Mayor Dave Bing Medical Update Statement from Robert Warfield, Director of Communications," March 24, 2012 <www.detroitmi.gov/News/tabid/3196/cte/ReadDefault/mid/4561/ArticleId/27/Default.aspx> (June 28, 2012). See also Hackney and Egan, "City could learn," and Leonard N. Fleming, "With Mayor sidelined, Lewis takes the ball," *Detroit News*, April 13, 2012.

31. City of Detroit, 2012–2013 Budget, Agency 37 Police Department.

For background on the fight against crime in Detroit, the nation's most violent big city, see George Hunter, Mike Wilkinson, Holly Fournier, "Police cuts loom as Detroit struggles to curb violence," *Detroit News*, June 8, 2012, A1.

To deal with reduction of 380 positions from a police force of about 2,600 (2,573), Michigan State Police troopers and Wayne County Sheriff's deputies were deployed to Detroit to aid with violent (felony) crime prevention and traffic enforcement. Previously, deputies had patrolled around Eight Mile Road. Under the Secondary Road Patrol Initiative, approved by the Detroit City Council in May 2012, deputies were allowed to patrol the city's other secondary roads or roads that are not highways or state trunk lines and enforce city ordinances, such as traffic violations. Funds for the extra patrols come out of state and county budgets. George Hunter, "Amid cuts, city gets police help," *Detroit News*, July 5, 2012, A1. For the Enhanced Police Reserve Program, requiring any person who applies to become a Detroit police officer to serve as a volunteer reservist, see George Hunter, "Police chief signs order to beef up reserve force," *Detroit News*, June 23, 2012, A1.

32. City of Detroit, 2012–2013 Budget, Agency 24 Fire Department.

33. For background on the Detroit Emergency Medical Service under the budgetary pay cuts and using outdated ambulances, see Tony Briscoe, "Overloaded staff frustrated by cuts, lack of resources," *Detroit News*, August 16, 2012, A1.

34. Melanie Scott Dorsey, "Detroit Fire Department gets $22.5M grant to preserve jobs," *Detroit Free Press*, July 7, 2012, A4.

35. City of Detroit, 2012-2013 Budget, Agency 39 Recreation Department.

36. Leonard N. Fleming, "Bing says $15M in donations will keep city recreation centers open," *Detroit News*, August 23, 2012, A1, and Cecil Angel, "Private money to fund rec centers," *Detroit Free Press*, August 23, 2012 <LexisNexis>.

37. City of Detroit, 2012–2013 Budget, Agency 25 Department of Health and Wellness Promotion.

The transfer proceeded despite the city council's objections, but subject to the Institute honoring the department's collective bargaining agreement. Steve Pardo and Darren A. Nichols, "Health agency plan to proceed," *Detroit News*, September 29, 2012, A3. See also Mark Hicks, "Ruling: Detroit must honor Health Dept. contract," *Detroit News*, September 28, 2012, A7; Steve Pardo, "Detroit feuds over control of health services," *Detroit News*, September 24, 2012, A1; Matt Helms, "City Council to stop health agency plan," *Detroit Free Press*, September 19, 2012 <LexisNexis>; Steve Pardo,

"Detroit city union sue to block outsourcing," *Detroit News*, June 13, 2012, A6; Darren A. Nichols, "Health Dept. control at issue," *Detroit News*, May 17, 2012, A7.

38. City of Detroit, 2012–2013 Budget, Agency 21 Detroit Workforce Development Department.

39. City of Detroit, 2012–2013 Budget, Agency 30 Department of Human Services.

40. Act 336 of 1947. In November 2012, Michigan voters defeated a ballot proposal to enshrine collective bargaining rights for public and private employees in the state constitution.

41. A state trial court upheld the 10 percent pay cut and other benefit reductions for Detroit police officers. George Hunter, "Union chief: Detroit's cops looking elsewhere," *Detroit News*, September 20, 2012, A15. The Financial Stability Agreement apparently supercedes Act 312 of 1969, which provides for compulsory arbitration of labor disputes in Michigan municipal police and fire departments.

42. City of Detroit, Discussion Document, July 16, 2012. See also Matthew Dolan and Devlin Barrett, "Bomb Threats Rattle Detroit as Cuts Take Hold," *Wall Street Journal*, July 20, 2012, A3; Monica Davey, "Detroit Mayor Confirms Cuts to Workers' Pay and Benefits," *New York Times*, July 19, 2012, A15; Suzette Hackney and Matt Helms, "Bing slashes city workers' pay, lays off hundreds more," *Detroit Free Press*, July 19, 2012, A1; Darren A. Nichols, "Divided Detroit council rejects imposed contracts," *Detroit News*, July 18, 2012, A1; Matt Helms, "Despite Detroit council's vote, union cuts on the way," *Detroit Free Press*, July 18, 2012, A1; Darren A. Nichols and Steve Pardo, "Council to weigh wage cut proposal," *Detroit News*, July 16, 2012, A3; Suzette Hackney, Gina Damron, Cecil Angel, "Detroit police union is preparing for a fight against 10% pay cuts," *Detroit Free Press*, July 14, 2012, A1; Darren A Nichols, "Financial board OKs cuts to union contracts," *Detroit News*, July 13, 2012, A1; Matt Helms and Suzette Hackney, "Financial board OKs Bing plan to slash pay for union workers," *Detroit Free Press*, July 13, 2012, A1.

43. Steven T. Khalil, "Detroit Could Collect Savings from Privatized Garbage Pickup," Mackinac Center for Public Policy, Michigan Privatization Report, No. 2000-04, Winter 2001 (Michigan Privatization Report), 8–9, at 8.

In June 2011, Mayor Bing considered privatizing garbage collection to improve performance and save an estimated $14 million annually. Darren A. Nicols, "Privatized trash pickup weighed," *Detroit News*, June 10, 2011, A4.

For an analysis of the benefits of residential refuse collection in Minneapolis and Phoenix, which have competitive systems in which municipal service providers compete with private, for-profit firms, see John Rehfuss, *Contracting Out in Government: A Guide to Working with Outside Contractors to Supply Public Services* (San Francisco: Jossey-Bass, 1989), 45. See generally Stephen Goldsmith, *Governing by Network: The New Shape of the Public Sector* (Washington, DC: Brookings Institution, 2004) and John Hanrahan, *Government by Contract* (New York: Norton, 1983).

44. Ronald Freeland, "DDOT has failed Detroit, but it is improving, CEO says," *Detroit News*, May 25, 2012, A17, and Ronald Freeland, "DDOT bus service getting better," *Detroit Free Press*, May 24, 2012, A14. See also Matt

Helms, "Bing boosts bus plan," *Detroit Free Press*, May 1, 2012, A3, and Josh Katzenstein, "Officials target timeliness, add service to 4 busy lines," *Detroit News*, May 1, 2012, A3. But see Transportation Riders United, Broken Promises: DDOT Still Failing to Provide Adequate Bus Services, April 24, 2012.

45. Matt Helms, "DDOT's new CEO aims to stabilize service for city," *Detroit Free Press*, February 23, 2012, A5.

46. See, e.g., Matt Helms, "DDOT cuts mean longer wait time," *Detroit Free Press*, March 29, 2012, A3.

47. Darren A. Nichols, "Detroit's bus system improved, firm reports," *Detroit News*, September 11, 2012, A3.

48. City of Detroit, 2012–2013 Executive Budget Summary, A6. The Detroit City Charter restricts the sale of buses and relevant assets, unless approved by a majority of voters. City of Detroit, Charter of the City of Detroit, Section 7-1104, January 1, 2012.

49. Wendell Cox, "Privatization Should Drive Detroit Transportation," Michigan Privatization Report, 16, 17. Any franchise for bus services is subject to the revocation, at will, by the city council, unless approved by a three-fifths super-majority of voters. City of Detroit, Charter of the City of Detroit, Section 7-1104.

50. Darren A. Nichols and Christine MacDonald, "Outage puts negative spotlight on Detroit's aging lighting dept.," *Detroit News*, June 11, 2011, A1, and Steve Neavling, "Power restored, but real fix will cost millions," *Detroit Free Press*, June 11, 2011, A1.

51. Happold Consulting, Phase One: Research and Priorities: Policy Audit Topics: City Systems-Infrastructure, Transportation & Sustainability, Detroit Works Project, December 22, 2012, 4.3 (Energy Public Lighting Department).

52. City of Detroit, 2012–2013 Executive Budget Summary, A5. The City Charter restricts the granting of any public utility franchise for public lighting that is not subject to revocation, at will, by the city council, unless approved by a three-fifths super-majority of voters. Furthermore, the city cannot sell any property needed to continue the operation of the municipal public utility furnishing lighting, unless approved by a majority of voters. City of Detroit, Charter of the City of Detroit, Section 7-905.

53. City of Detroit, Press Release, "Mayor Bing Unveils Public Lighting Strategy for City of Detroit," August 10, 2012. See also Suzette Hackney, "Bing rolls out plan to get lights on," *Detroit Free Press*, August 11, 2012 <LexisNexis>.

54. City of Detroit, 2012–2013 Executive Budget Summary, A5.

55. But see Ronald D. Utt, "The Power to Privatize," Michigan Privatization Report, 19 and 24, and Ronald D. Utt, "Time to Privatize Detroit's Public Lighting Department," April 9, 2002 <http://www.mackinac.org/article> (December 7, 2011). See generally John D. Donahue, *The Privatization Decision: Public Ends, Private Means* (New York: Basic, 1989) and E. S. Savas, *Privatization: The key to Better Government* (Chatham, NJ: Chatham House, 1987).

56. See, e.g., Christine MacDonald, "Detroit seeks fraction of $200M owed," *Detroit News*, September 19, 2009, A1.

In May 2012, the city council adopted a new ordinance, the Emergency Services Cost Recovery, that enables the city to seek reimbursement for hospital transport services provided by the Fire Department's Emergency Medical Services Division from parties who bear responsibility.

57. The statistics in this paragraph are from Report of Detroit Financial Review Team, 4 and Citizens Research Council of Michigan (CRCM), Legacy Costs and Indebtedness of the City of Detroit, Report 373, December 2011, 10–12. A report by Foster McCollum White & Associates, City of Detroit Fiscal and Operational Plan and Regional Governance Model, n.d., 7, placed Detroit's long-term liabilities at $15.83 billion. See generally, CRMC, Legacy Costs.

58. City of Detroit, Discussion Document, July 16, 2012, 4.
It is uncertain how the Governmental Accounting Standards Board's new pension rules that, among other things, limit the rate of return on future investments that pension funds can assume for accounting purposes, will impact on Detroit's unfunded pension obligations. Governmental Accounting Standards Board (GASB), Statement No. 67 of the GASB, Financial Reporting for Pension Plans, No. 327-B. June 2012 and GASB, Press Release, "GASB Improves Pension Accounting and Financial Reporting Standards," June 25, 2012 <www.gasb.org/cs> (June 28, 2012). See also Michael A. Fletcher, "New rules expose huge funding gaps for public pensions," *Washington* Post, August 17, 2012, A12, and Mary Williams Walsh, "New Pension Rules Seek Disclosure," *New York Times*, June 25, 2012, B1.

59. See, e.g., Fitch Rating, Press Release, "Fitch Downgrades Detroit, MI, ULTGO's to 'CCC'; LTGOs & COPs to 'CC'; Maintains COPs on Negative Watch," June 12, 2012. See also Michael Corkery, "Oakland Angles for an Exit," *Wall Street Journal*, July 24, 2012, C3.

60. City of Detroit, Office of the Auditor General, Analysis of the Mayor's 2011–2012 Proposed Budget, 29-33.

61. Michigan Constitution Section 24. Detroit is also obligated under its City Charter (Charter of the City of Detroit, January 1, 2012 Section 11-101.3) and pre-July 2012 union contracts to pay pensions earned by its municipal employees.

62. See, e.g., Michael Cooper and Mary William Walsh, "Leading Way, 2 Cities Pass Pension Cuts," *New York Times*, June 7, 2012, A1.

4

Rightsizing Detroit's Public Sector

The need to engage in land-use planning and rightsize city government and refocus its essential services, led Mayor Dave Bing to propose his signature initiative, the Detroit Works Project (the Project). Bing hoped the Project would provide more cost-effective public service delivery for Detroit's sprawling, but shrinking, population. In addition to striving to restore fiscal sanity to Detroit, he struggled with how to calibrate and allocate municipal services and target public-sector resources into more dense, stable communities. To do this, Bing realized that the city could not eliminate energy infrastructure, such as shutting water lines and removing street lights, and discontinue services, such as garbage pickup, to depopulated areas to force relocations. Even if funds were available to provide financial incentives, which they were not, moving residents to denser, more stable neighborhoods would prove a difficult, if not impossible, obstacle to effective land-use planning and rightsizing Detroit's public sector. Furthermore, in blocks containing some occupied residences, the cost savings gained by eliminating energy infrastructure, for example, street lights, are problematic and, at best, modest. Street lights, among other types of physical infrastructure, operate on a fixed grid. Removing street lights in depopulated areas would adversely impact the entire system.[1]

As discussed in this chapter, the Project unfolded in four steps: genesis; listening and learning; implementation of a short-term action plan; and finally, an unveiling of a long-term action plan. At present, it is uncertain how the municipal government can reconfigure services to accommodate its downsized, widely scattered population in an era of fiscal austerity. The likelihood of success in creating an operationally efficient city seems tough to achieve.

Realizing that physical revitalization, specifically livable neighborhoods, also requires economic growth, human capital remediation, and innovation in productive use of land, the 2012 long-term plan, the Detroit Strategic Framework Plan, also set forth visionary strategic recommendations in these areas, which are briefly considered in this chapter. My analysis of efforts to increase jobs and promote economic development is examined in chapters 6 and 7. The possibilities for fostering innovation in productive use of vacant land are discussed in chapter 8.

At present, the 2012 long-range plan seems to have succeeded in addressing and overcoming a legacy of suspicion and distrust involving any municipal planning effort. It achieved another significant objective of gaining a consensus that Detroit as a smaller place could be a better place. Beyond these goals, it likely will sit on the shelf, with low odds for comprehensive implementation, at least in the foreseeable future.

The Project's Genesis

Originally, Bing and his advisors talked big. They envisioned a true transformation, the need to take a quantum leap, involving a fundamental restructuring of population and public services they regarded as essential to the city and its future. Bing wanted to divert public funds for essential services, such as public safety and street lighting, from struggling neighborhoods by concentrating the sprawling city's plummeting population into its healthiest areas, presumably to reduce municipal expenses. Seemingly, however, his staff undertook no analysis of the specific cost savings to be achieved by decreasing or eliminating services in vacant areas of Detroit.

Bing's plan was not new. In 1993, for example, the city's then ombudsman Marie Farrell-Donaldson, in essence, suggested that the most blighted parts of Detroit should be closed down.[2] After residents were relocated from these areas to those that had more life in them, the empty houses and other structures could be demolished and the abandoned areas fenced off. By redirecting services to more densely populated areas, the city could provide essential public functions at a cost it could afford.

Fast-forward to 2010. Under Bing's initial, so-called "hard" approach, underpopulated neighborhoods would witness, for example, reduced garbage pickup, and the turning off (or at least the non-repair) of street lights.[3] In September 2010, Bing told reporters that residents who remained in these desolate neighborhoods could "have some problems if they decide to live there."[4]

In formulating the Project to steer people to "better" neighborhoods, rather than leaving them scattered throughout the 139-square-mile city, early on, Bing reasoned, "We've got to pick those core communities, those core neighborhoods" to sustain and preserve.[5] Furthermore, he asserted, "Key to our comeback is density—get as many people as you can into the areas we're [the public sector's] going to reinvest in."[6]

No resident would be forced to move, but those who remain in areas outside the population clusters, Bing indicated, "[N]eed to understand that they're not going to get the kind of services they require. We're going to be encouraging them to move and put themselves in a better situation. . . . They are much better off moving into a more dense area so that we can provide them with the services they need: that would be water, sewer, lighting, public safety—all of that. We think that getting our city to be more dense with its population is the right route." As to the neighborhoods targeted for public-sector expenditures, they will be relatively stable, albeit with some foreclosed and vacant property. Bing continued, "We want to make sure that before those neighborhoods deteriorate much more, we give them support."[7] Implementing a plan to meet Bing's objectives proved, however, more difficult than his words would have indicated.

Listening and Learning

To prepare residents for the new realities and the implementation of the "hard" plan, through a series of neighborhood and citywide town hall meetings that thousands attended between September 2010 and May 2011, Bing and his aides sought community input on plans to reshape the city.[8] They talked about identifying seven to nine areas that would encompass some two-thirds of Detroit's 139 square miles, where the city would continue to provide the full range of municipal functions, including garbage collection. At the same time, the city would pull back, if not eliminate, various public services from more sparsely populated areas.[9] As floated, Bing wanted to encourage residents to migrate from desolate areas swallowed by crime, poverty, and blight into steadier neighborhoods. With strengthened public schools as well as improved public safety and other community services, these more stable, if not vibrant, areas would concentrate Detroit's population, enabling the funneling of limited public-sector dollars to the city's most viable swaths.

At the initial town hall meetings in the fall of 2010, residents resisted Bing's efforts to virtually shut down blighted areas, by reducing, if not eliminating, public services. Evidencing skepticism of anything foisted on them, Detroiters did not want to be told where they should live. Furthermore, city employee unions were upset at the prospect of reduced public services. Consolidating services by redirecting residents to seven or nine neighborhoods that had not lapsed into blight would mean additional municipal job losses.

History also played a role in residents' resistance to Bing's proposal. Detroiters were skeptical about city-led planning endeavors. Past efforts to move residents proved complicated in Detroit, cost millions of dollars, exacerbated blight, and left neighborhoods in limbo.[10]

Over the decades, Detroit has had a bitter history of urban renewal and forced relocations, particularly from established black neighborhoods. The city bulldozed the Black Bottom neighborhood, a predominantly African American area, in the 1960s for the Chrysler Freeway and the Lafayette Park residential development. Hundreds of residents were relocated to public housing projects. In the 1980s, the city moved thousands of Poletown residents on the Hamtramck border for a General Motors' plant. More than 4,200 people were relocated and some 600 businesses were forced to sell.[11] It cleared Rivertown in the 1990s for a failed plan to cluster casinos near the Detroit River.

Two other notable efforts proved futile. An attempt to build a safety buffer near the Coleman A. Young International Airport cost at least $28 million and has lasted more than seventeen years, not the eighteen months as promised. The city hoped to buy out 500 property owners; at present, it still has some 200 parcels to go.

Detroit spent $19 million buying land for a development-ready industrial park, the I-94 Industrial Park, on the eastside. In 1999, the city mapped plans for the industrial park to spark an economic rebirth in the area by attracting a cluster of new warehouses and manufacturing businesses. The city bought out 200 property owners, razing their houses. As of 2011, it still needed to purchase another 90 parcels, mostly vacant lots and abandoned structures. The industrial park attracted but one tenant and the expectation of new economic development never happened.

Given this background, as city officials solicited residents' views, the initial, often chaotic town hall meetings often degenerated into "gripe sessions and shouting matches."[12] Mutual recriminations abounded. City leaders claimed that The Kresge Foundation (Kresge) botched the process and sowed distrust. Rip Rapson blamed top Bing aides for bungling the town hall meetings. The city planning department cold-shouldered Toni L. Griffin, a well-regarded urban planner Kresge hired to work for the city and guide the Project. Kresge funded Griffin's salary but she served in Detroit's Planning and Development Department. She spearheaded the Project's planning process prior to the town hall meetings. City leaders felt that Griffin relied too heavily on consultants and her own data-driven approach, apparently often brushing aside work already done by local groups.

Subsequently, in 2011, the meetings were restructured, keeping complaints, grievances, and protests under better control. City officials calmly answered attendees' questions. Disagreements or challenges were not allowed.[13]

Reconfiguring the Project

Ultimately, Bing scaled back his ambitious plan to rightsize the city and its public functions. Because the city lacked legal authority to terminate services to residents who refused to move, the focus turned to improving services in "better" neighborhoods.[14] The hard approach turned into a soft one, with Bing separating the project into two tracks: a short-term action plan and a long-term plan.

The Project's Short-Term Action Plan

In July 2011, Bing unveiled his interim plan. Recast as a "short-term intervention strategy,"[15] the plan sought to reshape the delivery of city services. In attempting to make public functions more efficient and save certain neighborhoods, it represented the Project's first concrete measure. In announcing his overhaul of how the cash-strapped city would serve residents, Bing stated, "We can't continue to do business the same way we have. We must be smarter about how we align our resources. Our entire city will benefit from this new market approach of service delivery."[16]

Bing and his city hall team, drawing on consultants' research[17]— specifically, two analyses, a residential physical condition analysis and a market value analysis—divided Detroit into three basic market types: steady, transitional, and distressed. Designations were largely made based on the condition of an area's real estate, including housing stock, median home sales prices, number of foreclosures, and the amount of vacant land and the number of abandoned structures. The short-term action plan did not treat all neighborhoods equally in terms of public services. Rather, services provided would depend on a neighborhood's market type.

To implement the short-term plan based on market analyses, in July 2011, the mayor's staff released a block-by-block, color-coded analysis of the city. It tagged neighborhoods as steady, transitional, or distressed. These labels would guide city planners in targeting tens of millions of dollars in funding, with all neighborhoods, regardless of their market type, continuing to receive a minimum level of basic public services. No community would go without essentials, such as police, fire, and emergency medical services. These service basics, as well as trash collection, would continue to be delivered equally throughout the city. No part of the city would be shut down. No residents would be asked or required to move. Bing would continue to demolish thousands of abandoned (and dangerous) homes and buildings, but be more selective in targeting these funds.

In the steady market type neighborhoods, which represent only a fraction of the city, homes are in good physical condition, with the majority being owner-occupied and having the highest housing prices. These healthier neighborhoods with relatively stable populations would receive more of certain services, such as street light repairs and tree trimming, and active code enforcement, than blighted areas. More economic development funds, such as commercial corridor improvements, would flow to steady neighborhoods, with medium- and low-economic development expenditures for transitional and distressed areas, respectively.

Transitional market type areas have a relatively high presence of bank-owned properties and a mix of rental and owner-occupied homes. Some population losses had occurred in transitional neighborhoods. These locales would see a rapid response to any blighting influences, including more building demolitions and board-ups of abandoned homes and buildings.

Distressed market type areas show signs of long-term physical decline, a near absence of market activity in real estate transactions, high vacancy rates, few amenities, such as stores, and high concentrations of vacant land. In concept, seemingly but not in practice, these areas would see the most demolitions of blighted structures with more funds expended to clear vacant lots than in other market type areas. Distressed neighborhoods would see low expenditures for road improvements and street lighting.

Throughout Detroit, problems exist with illegal dumping on vacant land. To prevent (or at least, lessen) illegal dumping, the city would try to have debris cleared in a more timely manner. Instead of collecting bulk trash four times a year, Department of Public Works' trucks would be sent more often to distressed areas rather than those considered steady.

In rolling out the soft plan, Bing designated three demonstration areas, not the entire city, for a test run. The three areas are as follows: Hubbard Farms/Southwest; Bagley/Detroit Golf Club/Green Acres/ Palmer Woods/Sherwood Forest/University District; and Boston– Edison/North End/Virginia Park. Each area contains the three market types, characterized by a cross section of neighborhoods from vibrant business corridors and abandoned buildings, to immigrant enclaves, to historic districts, to stable family-owned and occupied homes and burnt-out residences, to test the various service delivery models. In short, each of the three designated demonstration areas offers a mix of the best the city has to offer along with pockets in dire need of attention. However, the three areas did not see an influx of additional services, only a reallocation of services.

The modest trial run tested processes related to service delivery, and its allocation, on relatively few people as a learning experiment. The short-term intervention strategy, as a test, would hopefully show results that could benefit everybody.[18]

City officials tracked data on a six-month cycle and assessed service delivery to determine whether to expand the program citywide. The first analysis of the triage approach reported a rise in "market confidence" among residents and private entities in the three demonstration areas.[19]

In implementing the short-term plan, unofficial and official changes occurred. Unofficially, in neighborhoods designated as distressed within the three demonstration areas, the city stopped or curtailed the demolition of abandoned residences and other buildings. It also neglected infrastructure maintenance, such as street lighting as well as tree trimming.[20] Although not broken out by neighborhood market type, in the three demonstration areas, officially, in the first six months, the city refurbished a total of seventy-one bus stops, repaired more than 9.5 miles of streets, and repaired or replaced some 2,000 street lights.[21] Also, in addition to these tepid efforts, to improve relationships with residents, the city held sixteen meetings with community leaders in the three demonstration areas.

To improve the market value of homes in parts of the three demonstration areas, the city formed a partnership with Citizens Bank to provide homeowners with matching funds to make exterior home repairs.[22] Within the short-term plan's first six months, 157 households in the three areas benefited from the $1.625-million program. Homeowners applied for a grant, completed the renovation, and Citizens reimbursed them for one-half of a project's cost, up to $10,000.

The city began ending subsidies to largely gone, distressed areas. In coming years, Detroit will spend tens of millions of dollars in federal funds to improve neighborhoods, including community development and neighborhood stabilization grants. In an effort to be more strategic, the city, for example, will provide funds for new or renovated housing only in its most physically stable neighborhoods or areas with potential to achieve that status, provided the blight has not reached a tipping point.[23] Conversely, areas in long-term decline with properties of little value will receive attention only if they are near strong or physically stable neighborhoods. For example, Detroit's Senior Emergency Home Repair program, funded by federal Community Development Block Grants, providing home repair grants of up to $12,000, and the city's Minor Home Repair grants of up to $25,000 to address health and safety issues in residents' homes will not go to those in distressed areas. The city will not approve builders getting Michigan State Housing Authority and the US Department of Housing and Urban Development (HUD) grants and tax credits in blighted neighborhoods. Furthermore, the city will not provide new sewer lines, sidewalks, or street lights for new developments in these areas. In sum, in making funding decisions, Detroit will seek to increase the size of denser, more stable areas, defund distressed areas, and keep declining neighborhoods from spreading.

Federal Government Expresses Confidence in Bing's Plan

In July 2011, the federal government expressed its faith in Bing's plan to reshape the city by growing selected, strong neighborhoods. As part of the federal Strong Cities, Strong Communities Initiative,[24] under the US Department of Housing and Urban Development, the federal government infused the city with federal experts in housing, transportation, health care, and jobs from various agencies, including HUD, the Transportation, Labor, and Commerce Departments as well as the Small Business Administration. Detroit was one of six cities nationwide, including Cleveland, Chester, PA, Fresno, CA, Memphis, and New Orleans, to receive the assistance of federal workers for up to two years under the initiative.

The program aims to help revive these cities and neighborhoods where federal money has often gone unspent or squandered without having a significant impact. In particular, Detroit has long faced a problem of returning appropriated federal funds that were not spent in a timely manner. As part of the initiative, city officials in four departments met regularly with visiting federal experts to help Detroit gain the maximum benefit from federal funds by disbursing these monies effectively.

Long-Term Planning

In December 2011, the long-term phase of the Project was re-launched.[25] With fresh funding from The Kresge, Kellogg, and Ford Foundations, the long-term planning for the Project, unlike the short-term aspect, occurred outside of city hall.

The long-term phase included a revamped organizational structure. A thirteen-member steering committee, appointed by the mayor, with members from the business, nonprofit, government, and philanthropic sectors, oversaw the Project's long-term planning. Chaired by the president and CEO of the Detroit Economic Growth Corp., a quasi-public body, the steering committee managed, advised, and provided guidance to two teams. Toni Griffin, whom the Project brought back in 2012, headed the technical team, and Dan Pitera, Executive Director, Detroit Collaborative Design Center (a multidisciplinary, nonprofit organization dedicated to renewing the city by revitalizing its neighborhoods), at the University of Detroit Mercy School of Architecture, led the community engagement team, which implemented a broader engagement process than had taken place previously. The community engagement team undertook a massive project to involve key constituencies and residents in the process so as to try to clear the air of suspicion and distrust. Seeking "real" engagement, it held community meetings, open houses, and other events to acquaint Detroiters with the plan's ideas and gain feedback, ostensibly used in preparing the final recommendations. Researching and analyzing the city's physical, social, and economic landscape, the two teams, blending technical analysis and community input, worked to produce the 2012 Detroit Strategic Framework Plan[26] that would serve as the roadmap for Detroit's future.

The Mayor's Advisory Task Force served in an advisory capacity to the steering committee, providing feedback about the Project.[27] Appointed by the mayor, the fifty-five-member task force consists of residents as well as representatives from community groups, faith-based and nonprofit organizations, and the business and foundation communities.

Planning for the rightsizing of public services and improving neighborhood stability, among other elements, took place in the context of Detroit's fiscal crisis, as analyzed in chapter 3, that resulted in a substantial decrease in municipal expenditures. The Project's long-term plan, a vision of what Detroit would look like with policy recommendation and implementation strategies, was unveiled in January 2013.[28]

In presenting a vision of a smaller, more sustainable city, the [draft] long-term plan built on the short-term action plan for reallocating services but continuing to provide a minimal level of essential services, such as public safety, to all areas of the city. With respect to expenditures on various services, for example, water, waste, energy, and road repairs, the plan envisioned a triage system with various strategies keyed to three neighborhood types, called framework zones, based on existing conditions and level of property abandonment: areas with little or no vacancies; areas with moderate vacancies; high-vacancy areas with much abandonment.[29] To promote a range of sustainable densities, priorities were assigned to various strategies. For example, stronger areas would be targeted for new retail and residential efforts. Mostly abandoned areas would be singled out for more green strategies. It divided the strategies for renewal and maintenance of city infrastructure and systems, such as energy, road repairs, and water, which require significant, annual investments with twenty- to fifty-year timespans, into one of five categories: upgrade and maintain; renew and maintain; reduce and maintain; maintain only; replace, repurpose, or decommission.[30] Maintenance would be reduced over time in areas where population is unlikely to return, with maintenance, renewal, and upgrading concentrated in more densely populated areas.

The long-range plan not only offered recommendations for more efficient public service delivery and infrastructure expenditures, but also proposed land-use reconfiguration. Some surplus vacant land, it recommended, would be used for infrastructure support, thereby providing three benefits: reducing maintenance costs for system upkeep; providing productive uses for and maintenance of land to reduce blight; and offering potential amenity space for residents. The proposed landscape systems for more vacant areas would include "blue infrastructure," such as rainwater-retention ponds designed to reduce stress on existing storm water–sewer systems. Reforestation, among other "green infrastructure" strategies, would create buffers against freeways and industrial areas.[31]

Realizing that jobs will play a significant, if not a determinant, role in the city's future, the plan also emphasized economic development and job creation, as part of a comprehensive strategy. Following its land-use roots, it focused on the creation of seven primary employment districts as the vehicle to attempt leverage of unique geographic assets within each so as to support sustainable economic growth.[32] The planners also urged support for local entrepreneurship, minority business ownership, improved workforce development, and enhanced transportation options.

The plan, however, lacked any type of funding mechanism for implementing its specific recommendations. However, The Kresge Foundation pledged $100 million over the next five years to assist in implementing the plan. Furthermore, a push will likely occur to fund pilot projects to start soon and produce quick results, as a springboard for obtaining additional resources from foundations, the federal government, corporations, and private investors.

Some Policy Questions

Focusing on narrower questions of where to channel scarce public-sector, resources, Detroit needs to consolidate neighborhoods to retain and attract middle-class residents by improving public services in stronger areas where there is hope. With fewer people than its infrastructure and public safety, among other services, were designed for (some 1.8 million), left to pay (some 700,000), some type of rationalization must occur. A need exists for a development pattern based on a downtown core and a network of viable neighborhoods with a strong community identity and local groups. The city must steer funds for public services and for new and rehabilitative developments, both residential and commercial, to reinforce stronger districts, ones having the best odds of thriving. Concentrating Detroit's scarce public resources in areas to maintain or enhance property values will hopefully generate new tax revenues for the city. Future mayors and city council members will lead the charge and gather support for focusing public services and reconfiguring land use. However, actions taken to address Detroit's shrinkage raise difficult issues of adopting and sustaining a viable national strategy, in the context of many vulnerable and impoverished urban residents. In addition, seven of the nine city council members will be elected from new voting districts, beginning in November 2013, with the two remaining council members continuing to run at-large.[33] The seven council members, who will reside in and answer to their neighbors in their respective geographical districts, will be more likely to defend their turf and oppose service cutbacks than the at-large members.

Even the "soft" short-term intervention plan, as expanded citywide in the long-term plan, raises a number of complex institutional questions. Characterizing areas as "distressed" or with much abandonment presents negative consequences. The classification will hurt real estate values. Potential investors and homeowners will likely not want to purchase and rehabilitate houses in such areas. The designation will also impact on insurers writing homeowner policies. They will be less likely to want to insure homes in distressed neighborhoods. Reduced street lighting in an area may encourage individuals and groups to commit crimes. Families will feel less safe from criminals, who will have a better idea where to go to commit crimes.

Although Mayor Bing denies he has a secret, long-term plan to relocate residents from underpopulated areas to more viable ones, reducing certain services, even if basic public functions are maintained, sends a message that the targeted neighborhoods will be cleared, eventually. However, for those who have lived in a community for decades, residing in areas where their nearest neighbor may be blocks away, the lure of better public services, safer streets, and more convenient shopping, among other amenities, may not serve as sufficient incentives for relocation. Lacking funds for financial incentives, it is problematic how the city can encourage people to move out of the weakest, the emptiest neighborhoods into "better" ones, the strongest and most viable, with some type of voluntary housing swap system allowing residents to relocate at little or no cost. In the end, it may be difficult, if not impossible, for the city to create the desired density and concentrate its limited public resources in hopefully safer, more manageable high-population areas.

In assessing the likelihood of relocating the one or the few last remaining homeowners on a block to move, one expert offered a negative appraisal, concluding it will "continue to be a difficult one." He reasoned:

> Given the history of urban renewal and the national controversy over eminent domain, any attempt to compel those last home owners, such as the Detroit home owner in the last occupied home on her desolate block who told a reporter, "I refuse to move unless the Lord says so," is doomed to failure. In some cities, this issue will be rendered more sensitive by the painful reality that the remaining home owners in many of these areas are disproportionately African-American and are often old enough to have personal memories of their city's "Negro removal" efforts. While there are many owners who feel trapped in unmarketable houses and lack the money to move, helping them move is likely to be a slow process, hindered by the city's chronic shortage of financial resources.[34]

At present, it is also uncertain whether efforts to create denser neighborhoods, with enhanced public services, will bring the middle class back. According to Bing, "I think public safety is number one. A productive school system number two. Because without either one of those being effective and efficient, you can forget everything else."[35] However, barriers exist to attracting and retaining the middle class: high auto insurance rates; the lack of stores; and a dysfunctional public school district.

The next chapter examines efforts to assure the financial viability and increase the academic performance of the Detroit Public School District.

Notes

1. Besides network capacity, Terry Schwarz, "Re-Thinking the Places in Between: Stabilization, Regeneration, and Reuse" in *Rebuilding America's Legacy Cities: New Directions for the Industrial Heartland*, ed. Alan Mallach (New York: American Assembly, 2012), 180–181, advances other reasons for cities not to downsize existing physical infrastructure, including capital costs of removal and uncertain patterns of future growth and shrinkage. See also John Hoornbeck and Terry Schwarz, Sustainable Infrastructure in Shrinking Cities: Options for the Future, Center for Public Administration and Public Policy and Cleveland Urban Design Collaborative, Kent State University, July 2009, 2.

2. *Economist*, "Inner cities: Day of the bulldozer," 327:7810 (May 8, 1993): 33–34. See also David Usborne, "Motor City fights against fulfilling a death wish," *The Independent* (London), May 31, 1993, 12, and Rogers Worthington, "What to do with vacant city lots? 'Mothball' them, official says," *Chicago Tribune*, May 5, 1993, N13. See generally Witold Ryboznski, "Downsizing Cities," *Atlantic Monthly* 276:4 (October 1995): 36, 38, 46–48.

3. Christine MacDonald, "City eyes trash, water, lighting cuts," *Detroit News*, April 6, 2011, A1.

4. Quoted in Darren A. Nichols, "City revamps land use forums," *Detroit News*, September 16, 2010, A4. See also Bing quoted in Christine MacDonald, "Public parks forum on city's future," *Detroit News*, September 15, 2010, A3.

5. Quoted in Alex P. Kellogg, "Detroit's Smaller Reality," *Wall Street Journal*, February 27–28, 2010, A3.

6. Quoted in *Forbes*, "Detroit: City of Hope" 188:1 (July 18, 2011): 86–96, at 90.

7. Quoted in Jeff Gerritt, "Bing: Let's move Detroiters into the city's viable areas," *Detroit Free Press*, December 9, 2010, A1.

8. City of Detroit, News Release, "Mayor Bing Announces Community Meetings Concerning Land Use Plan," August 19, 2010 <www.detroitmi.gov/Departmentsand Agencies/CommunicationsandCreativeServices> (April 6, 2011).

See also Darren A. Nichols, "Mayor's plan to reshape Detroit enters next stage," *Detroit News*, September 24, 2010, A12; Naomi R. Patton, "Detroiters' relocation fears grab hold of forum," *Detroit Free Press*, September 23, 2010, A17; Darren A. Nichols, "Detroit Works Project forums declared success," *Detroit News*, September 23, 2010, A4; Christine MacDonald, "First step is to stop residents from leaving, mayor says," *Detroit News*, September 22, 2010, A8; Naomi R. Patton, "Bing gets some positive ideas, civil reception," *Detroit Free Press*, September 22, 2010, A6; Tammy Stables Battaglia, "Detroiters get productive at 3rd open meeting," *Detroit Free Press*, September 19, 2010, A15; Laura Berman, "Mayor's 'hellhole' remark stings," *Detroit News*, September 18, 2010, A3; Naomi R. Patton, "Detroit forum on land use tries new tack," *Detroit Free Press*, September 17, 2010, A8; Nichols, "City revamps;" MacDonald, "Public packs;" Steve Neavling, "'Our biggest obstacle is to get people to believe,'" *Detroit Free Press*, September 15, 2010, A5.

9. See, e.g., Matthew Dolan, "Less Than a Full-Service City," *Wall Street Journal*, December 11–12, 2010, A3.

10. Christine MacDonald, "Recent city relocation projects fall short," *Detroit News*, March 9, 2011, A1. On the failure of post-World War II urban planning in Detroit, focusing on the interaction of redevelopment and racial issues, see June Manning Thomas, *Redevelopment and Race: Planning a Finer City in Postwar Detroit* (Baltimore: John Hopkins, 1997).

11. John J. Bukowozyk, "The Poletown Case and the Future of Detroit's Neighborhoods," *Michigan Quarterly Review* 25:2 (Spring 1986): 449–458, and John J. Bukowozyk, "The Decline and Fall of a Detroit Neighborhood: Poletown vs. G.M. and the City of Detroit," *Washington & Lee Law Review* 41:1 (Winter 1984): 49–76.

12. Matthew Dolan, "Revival Bid Pits Detroit vs. Donor," *Wall Street Journal*, July 2–3, 2011, A1.

13. Hunter Morrison and Margaret Dewar, "Planning in America's Legacy Cities: Toward Better, Smaller Communities after Decline" in *Rebuilding America's Legacy Cities*, 124–125.

14. For background on the current challenge of land-use planning in Detroit, see Monica Davey, "An Odd Challenge for Planners: How to Shrink a City," *New York Times*, April 6, 2011, A14. For seven lessons for practicing urban planners in shrinking cities, see Morrison and Dewar, "Planning in America's Legacy Cities," in *Rebuilding America's Legacy Cities*, 120–134. See also Corry Buckwalter Berkooz, "Repurposing Detroit: A resilient city launches a far-reaching planning initiative," *Planning* 76:9 (November 2010): 26–31.

15. Detroit Works Project (DWP), DWP: Neighborhood Analysis & Short-term Action Strategy: An Evidence-Based Strategy for Detroit Neighborhoods, n.d., and DWP, Press Release, "Short-Term Intervention Strategy," July 27, 2011 <www.detroitworksproject.com/2011/07/27/short-term-intervention-strategy> (August 30, 2011). See also Christine MacDonald, "Details snag Bing plan," August 12, 2011, A4; Matthew Dolan, "Detroit Mayor Scales Back His Overhaul Plan, for Now," *Wall Street Journal*, July 29, 2011, A5; Darren A. Nichols and Leonard N. Fleming, "Bing ready to make 'hard decisions' to revitalize neighborhoods," *Detroit News*, July 29, 2011, A6; Christine MacDonald, "Detroit services to depend on neighborhood condition," *Detroit News*, July 28, 2011, A1; Suzette Hackney and Steve Neavling, "Bing's plan puts services

to test," *Detroit Free Press*, July 28, 2011, A1; Darren A. Nichols, "Optimism, fear over Bing's plans," *Detroit News*, July 28, 2011, A9; Christine MacDonald, "Bing's plan to remake Detroit delayed," *Detroit News*, June 15, 2011, A1.

16. Quoted in MacDonald, "Detroit services."

17. According to Hackney and Neavling, "Bing's plan," foundations, other non-profits, and federal funds paid for the $2.5 million spent in connection with the formulation of the short-term plan on the neighborhood market analyses, consultants' fees, and the prior community engagement component. The city's 2009 master plan, which embodied a citywide comprehensive long-range strategy based on ten neighborhood clusters, also served as a data point for the project. City of Detroit, Master Plan of Policies, n.d.

18. Heaster Wheeler, Co-chairman, Detroit Works Project Advisory Task Force, quoted in Nichols and Fleming, "Bing ready."

19. City of Detroit, Press Release, "Market Confidence on the Rise in 3 Demonstration Areas after 6 Months," March 14, 2012 <www.detroitmi.gov> (April 6, 2012).

20. Cecil Angel, "Neighbors left, now services disappear," *Detroit Free Press*, May 20, 2012, A1.

21. City of Detroit, Press Release, "Market Confidence." DWP, Short-Term Actions for the Detroit Works Project, Progress Reports, n.d. <www.detroitmi.gov/Departmentsand Agencies/MayorsOffice/Initiatives/Short-TermAct> (October 16, 2012) tracked the progress made in the three demonstration areas on a six-month cycle. See also Suzette Hackney, "Homeowners in a bind," *Detroit Free Press*, May 10, 2012, A3; Laura Berman, "'Progress' fuels city hopes," *Detroit News*, March 13, 2012, A3; Christine MacDonald, "City targets services to healthy neighborhoods," *Detroit News*, September 29, 2011, A1. The short-term plan also recorded two other notable achievements: rehabilitating residences and transforming commercial corridors. With federal and state housing funds, as well as money from the city of Detroit, thirteen houses were rehabilitated in Boston–Edison and sold to buyers meeting income and other criteria. Megha Satyanarayana, "Detroit neighborhood welcomes new resident after house is rehabilitated," *Detroit Free Press*, August 22, 2012 <LexisNexis). For a summary of the transformation occurring along the Livernois commercial corridor using public-sector money and private capital, with the city making targeted investments fitting with an overall redevelopment plan crafted by the community, see Jeff Gerritt, "Turning the corner on commercial corridors," *Detroit Free Press*, August 19, 2012 <LexisNexis>.

22. City of Detroit, Press Release, "Market Confidence." See also Christine MacDonald, "Citizens Bank announces $1.6M in grants for Detroit homes," *Detroit News*, August 22, 2011, <www.detroitmi.gov/Departmentsand Agencies/MayorsOffice/Initiative/ShortTerm> (June 28, 2012). The August 2011 announcement came three months after Citizens Bank settled a lawsuit with the US Department of Justice Civil Rights Division to avoid federal accusations of discrimination against minority residents in the Detroit metro area.

23. DWP, Press Release, "Short-Term Action Strategy of Detroit Works Project Taking Shape," September 29, 2011. See also Angel, "Neighbors left" and Rochelle Riley, "City finding a way to make Detroit Works actually work," *Detroit Free Press*, February 18, 2012, A8.

24. US Department of Labor, Press Release, "Obama administration launches Strong Cities, Strong Communities to support local development," July 11, 2011; Shaun Donovan, Secretary, US Department of Housing and Urban Development, "As Go American Cities and Regions, 'So Goes Our Country's Economic Future,'" July 11, 2011 <vsotd.com>. See also David Shepardson, "Fed program helps Detroit cut red tape," *Detroit News*, March 16, 2012, A3; Steve Neavling and Kathleen Gray, "U.S. puts faith in Bing renewal plan," *Detroit Free Press*, July 12, 2011, A1; Christine MacDonald, "'Strong Cities' plan to give Detroit fed help," *Detroit News*, July 12, 2011, A2; Deb Price and Karen Bouffard, "Federal government to help direct Detroit's rebuilding," *Detroit News*, July 8, 2011, A1.

In March 2012, President Obama signed an executive order that established the White House Council on Strong Cities, Strong Communities. Executive Order 13602, Establishing a White House Council on Strong Cities, Strong Communities, March 15, 2012, *Federal Register* 77:54 (March 20, 2012): 16131–16134.

25. DWP, "Project Team" <www.detroitworksproject.com/about-us-2/project-team> (March 29, 2012) and "FAQ" <www.detroitworksproject.com/faq-2> (October 17, 2012). See also Laura Berman, "Detroit Works' innovations create needed engagement," *Detroit News*, December 20, 2011, A3; John Gallagher, "Detroit Works planning effort is promoted," *Detroit Free Press*, December 13, 2011, C2; John Gallagher, "Detroit Works re-launched," *Detroit Free Press*, December 4, 2011, A1. For Dan Pitera's view of looking to Detroiters for guidance see his article, "Listen to the people turn unused land into upbeat plans," *Detroit Free* Press, April 1, 2012, A20.

26. DWP, Detroit Future City, Detroit Strategic Framework Plan, December 2012.

27. DWP, "Advisory Task Force" <www.detroitworksproject.com/about-us-2/advisory-task-force> (March 29, 2012). In addition, the mayor appointed an Interagency Working Group, DWP, "Interagency Working Group" <www.detroitworksproject.com/about-us-2/interagency-working> (April 4, 2012).

28. DWP, Strategic Framework Plan, 12–13, 30–31.

29. Ibid., 103, 107, 122–123. Land-use typologies, namely, neighborhoods, industrial, and landscape, would serve as the structure for future zoning. Designating areas best suited for neighborhoods, industrial, and landscape uses would provide an efficient, future land-use pattern in Detroit, the planners hoped.

30. Ibid., 176–177.

31. Ibid., 182–183, 186, 297–301.

32. Ibid., 59–71.

33. City of Detroit, Charter of the City of Detroit, January 1, 2012, Section 3-108.

34. Alan Mallach, "Depopulation, Market Collapse, and Property Abandonment: Surplus Land and Buildings in Legacy Cities" in *Rebuilding America's Legacy Cities*, 106.

35. Quoted in Stephen Moore, "The Weekend Interview with Dave Bing," *Wall Street Journal*, December 19–20, 2009, A11.

5

Reviving the Detroit
Public School District

Beginning in 2009, Michigan again sought to revive the Detroit Public School (DPS) district. Previously, Michigan had taken over the DPS district from 1999 to 2005, with an appointed school board and a chief executive officer. In 2004, Detroit voters decided to turn the public schools back to an elected board that was restored in 2006. By late 2008, the state realized serious financial and academic problems existed with the DPS system.

For decades, Detroiters had witnessed a beleaguered, even deteriorating public school district.[1] Detroit's schools were in need of significant improvement after years of mismanagement, marked by huge budget deficits, and continuous in-fighting between the school board and a parade of superintendents that obscured students' needs. Hope came for a substantial improvement in the performance of the DPS system with the appointment of an emergency financial manager in 2009, and an emergency manager, with even broader powers, in 2011, who was reappointed first as an emergency financial manager with more limited authority in 2012 and then as an emergency manager— pursuant to the 2012 Local Financial Stability and Choice Act, which became effective in March 2013.

Despite declining enrollments and revenues, progress on the financial front came more quickly than academic achievement gains. Through a strong turnaround plan, the district balanced its budget in its 2012 fiscal year, achieving its first annual operating surplus since 2002, and projected a balanced budget for fiscal year 2013. As discussed in this chapter, the two state-appointed managers rightsized the district, focusing on school closures and consolidations. It appears probable the district will continue on the path to financial viability, particularly with the enactment of the 2012 Local Financial Stability and Choice Act, despite enrollment declines. The two managers also sought to stem the loss of students and improve academic achievement—the latter a far more difficult task, resulting, in part, from some parents' disinterest in their children's education and the opposition of the teachers' union.

Michigan also intervened with the creation of the Education Achievement System (EAS), a statewide school district designed to revive "failing" schools, the bottom 5 percent of all Michigan schools. As its first step, to improve academic achievement and enhance student performance, the EAS took over fifteen low-performing Detroit public schools in the fall of 2012.

Detroit Public School District's Academic Failures

Detroit must significantly improve the academic performance of its public schools, a tough task. By the first decade of the twenty-first century, the DPS system had become the nation's worst urban school district. It ranked at the bottom of student achievement among America's big cities.

In 2009 and 2011, DPS students attained the nation's lowest scores in reading and math on the National Assessment of Educational Progress (NAEP) tests. These tests, administered every other year as part of the US Department of Education's Trial Urban District Assessment, allow cities to compare scores from a significant sampling of their students with other big cities as well as state and national NAEP scores.

On the 2009 NAEP reading test, 73 percent of DPS fourth-graders scored below basic, that is, they lacked fundamental reading skills (compared to 45 percent of all large-city students), 22 percent were at the basic level, and only 5 percent were proficient. Among DPS eighth-graders in 2009, 60 percent tested below the basic level (compared to 34 percent for all big-city students), 34 percent were at the basic level, and only 6 percent were proficient. The 2011 reading scores showed a slight, but not a statistically meaningful, improvement. Sixty-nine percent of DPS fourth-graders scored below basic; at the same time, 57 percent of eighth-graders scored below basic.[2]

On the 2009 NAEP math test, 69 percent of DPS fourth-grade students and 77 percent of its eighth-grade students failed to attain the basic level in contrast to 28 percent and 40 percent, respectively, of fourth- and eighth-grade students in the nation's largest cities. Showing some progress, although not a statistically meaningful improvement, the 2011 test found 66 percent of the Detroit fourth-grade students scored below the basic level; and 71 percent of its eighth-grade students failed to achieve the basic level.[3]

In addition to these abysmal scores on standardized tests, what can only be described as lethargy characterized DPS students prior to 2009. On any given day, some 16 percent of all DPS students were absent. The average high school student missed 46 school days; nearly 10 percent of high school students missed more than 100 school days.[4] These absences led, in part, to a high dropout rate. According to official statistics, only about 60 to 62 percent of DPS students graduate from the city's high schools.[5] Unofficially, the graduation rate may be substantially lower, perhaps as low as 25 percent.[6]

Along with the high dropout rate and the city's plummeting population, the DPS system experienced continued student enrollment losses in the first decade of the twenty-first century, seemingly with no clear end in sight. Enrollment fell from 162,000 students in the 2000–01 academic year to 66,700 plus 4,000 in charter schools by the fall of 2011, and to about 52,000 (51,674) plus those in charter schools and the schools operated by the Education Achievement Authority in the fall of 2012.[7] The downward trend resulted from multiple factors including the exodus of families from the city, a declining birth rate, low student performance, and the prevalence of crime in and around public schools. However, the enrollment decline exceeded the drop in the city's population.

Appointment of an Emergency Financial Manager

The year 2009 marked a turnaround not only in municipal government, as analyzed in chapter 3, but also in the DPS district. The state realized that the Detroit Public School system's finances were out of kilter, following years of mismanagement. Governor Jennifer M. Granholm (D) declared a state of financial emergency after a Michigan financial review team found that the district had failed to make strides to resolve its fiscal deficits.[8] Stripping the local school board's control over the system's budget, she appointed Robert C. Bobb as the emergency financial manager to take over the troubled school district's finances.[9] Governor Granholm hoped Bobb could erase the accumulated deficits that plagued the district and eliminate the deep-seated corruption and outright fraud that pervaded the system.

In taking over, Bobb, a veteran public administrator, faced seven years (2002–09) of deficits resulting from the failure to aggressively reduce spending and close largely vacant schools, as enrollment dropped. He was charged with developing and implementing a strategy to lessen, if not eliminate, an accumulated deficit that approached $220 million.

Before leaving at the end of June 2011, as his contract ran out, having been extended twice first in March 2010 and then in March 2011, Bobb tried to fix something that was broken for years. In the process, he angered countless students, parents, and teachers, especially by aggressively closing schools, as a result of dwindling enrollment.[10]

Bobb's achievements were many. He up-ended a culture of inertia and waste. Most notably, he closed fifty-nine schools, despite the pleas of those resistant to change. The school closures saved the system millions of dollars in annual expenses through reduced operating and maintenance costs. However, the decision to close schools, based on a number of criteria, including academic performance, demographic trends, facility condition, investment needs, and operating costs, represented a blow to the impacted neighborhoods that had significant emotional attachments to their local schools. In protesting school closings, parents and other residents unrealistically hoped that magically someone, somehow would come in and turn around half-empty, low-performing schools.

Bobb removed principals from 91 of 147 schools. His accord with the teachers' union gave principals more leverage in staffing decisions.

Focusing on improving student achievement, although, his ability to implement academic changes remained in doubt until, judicially sanctioned in March 2011,[11] Bobb instituted an extended school day requiring 120 minutes of reading and math daily for K–8 students and a double dose of algebra for ninth-graders. He implemented free, five-day-a-week summer school classes for all K–8 students, and for high school students whose families qualified for free or reduced-price school lunches to ensure that more students did not fall behind. Ending social promotion for low-performing students, he also aligned the district's curriculum to National Association of Educational Progress Standards and increased student testing to help children meet academic benchmarks.

To cut the district's expenses, Bobb sold surplus assets and outsourced bus, security, and custodial services. In addition to laying-off some 1,700 employees, including hundreds of administrators, to get a handle on "ghost" employees, he ordered all jobholders to show up in person to collect their paychecks or direct deposit stubs. He even fired members of his own security detail for overstating their overtime hours.

Bobb pressed for and obtained financial concessions totaling some $30 million from the teachers' union in December 2009,[12] as part of a three-year agreement that also included various managerial reforms, such as shared decision making, peer assistance and review, and comprehensive teacher evaluations. Although Detroit teachers made considerably less than suburban counterparts, he secured their agreement to defer a total of $10,000 in pay for two years and contribute more for their health insurance costs. Under the Termination Incentive Plan, which was subsequently ruled illegal, the deferred salary money went into a special account that allowed the district to use the funds to pay its bills. The district agreed to return the money when a teacher left the system. Balanced against these cuts to save money, Bobb, however, spent millions on financial and other consultants to clean up the fiscal mess left by prior superintendents.

Despite Bobb's deep cuts, the district remained steeped in red ink. As hard as he tried, he could not balance the system's budget. The $220 million accumulated deficit when Bobb arrived in 2009 ballooned to $327 million by 2011, because of unanticipated revenue declines. The more schools Bobb closed to save money, the more parents grew discouraged and pulled their children out of the system. Residents sought other communities to live in and other educational choices for their children. Fewer enrolled students resulted in less state funds, leading to even more school closings. The exodus of some 8,000 students in a year overshadowed any cost savings. For each departing student, Detroit lost some $7,300 in state money, an annual loss of $58.4 million,[13] thereby further crimping district funding and increasing the system's accumulated deficit.

To bridge the ever-widening budget gap, Bobb turned to short-term borrowing. For example, in March 2011, the district sold $231 million in short-term notes, through the Michigan Finance Authority, to fund operating costs through August 2011.[14] A pledge of a portion of the district's future state-aid revenue secured the repayment of the notes.

Appointment of an Emergency Manager

In July 2011, Roy S. Roberts,[15] an African American product of the Detroit public schools, a former General Motors vice president for North American vehicle sales, service, and marketing, took over as DPS's Emergency Manager, with a mandate to balance the district's books by 2016. Hired by Governor Rick Snyder,[16] Roberts scaled back Bobb's previously announced plans for school closings and charter conversions. With clear authority encompassing academic matters, Roberts initially reduced class sizes at most grade levels, specifically from thirty-three to thirty students in grades 4 and 5 and from thirty-eight to thirty-five students in grades 6–12, and expanded the pre-kindergarten program. However, he then increased class sizes for grades 4 and 5 back to thirty-three students and for grades 6–12 to thirty-eight students in the fall of 2012, thereby returning to the prior 2010–11 levels. It will take much larger classes than these, however, to trigger the various maximum class sizes.[17]

In 2012, Roberts modified the DPS district's summer school program to target 18,000 of its lowest performing students with one-on-one instruction in smaller classroom settings. The six-week program was mandatory for struggling K–8 students. A credit recovery program for grades 9–12 was offered to enable high school students to retake classes and stay on track for graduation.[18]

Like Mayor Bing, Roberts faced a significant obstacle to attain his fiscal objectives: salary and fringe benefit costs. To reduce spending and bring operating expenses in line with revenues, in 2011 he imposed a 10 percent wage cut (subsequently partially rescinded in a court settlement) on all district employees; took away teacher compensation for oversized classes; and revised the system's health, dental, life insurance, and vision plans to increase employee contributions.[19] The new 2012 contract, the Successor Collective Bargaining Agreement, imposed by Roberts under the 2011 emergency manager law, continues the 10 percent pay cut (with the exception of food service assistance staff); raises employees' share of dental insurance coverage and prescription co-pays; decreases maternity leave benefits; and reduces the amount of paid time elementary school teachers receive to prepare for class.[20] Because this contract took effect prior to the suspension of the 2011 emergency manager law in August 2012 and its repeal in November of that year by a ballot measure, it remains valid and binding. With the new 2012 legislation, the state-appointed manager will have the power to abrogate collective bargaining and impose new contractual terms on DPS employees.

To rightsize the number of personnel in the face of declining enrollment and revenues, Roberts reduced the district's employees by some 800 (853) from 10,122 to 9,269 in the 2011–12 fiscal year and cut another 2,000 workers the next fiscal year. The DPS district decreased its budget by nearly one-quarter from $1.04 billion to $754 million for its 2012–13 fiscal year.[21]

In addition to personnel cuts and wage and benefit reductions, to save money, Roberts rebid all the system's major contracts and decreased the top thirty central office positions, many filled with consultants, to seven. He also relocated the system's offices from leased space in three different buildings to one main location owned by the district.

To help further shrink the system's accumulated budget deficit and avoid additional drastic personnel and other cuts, in October 2011, Roberts completed a $245 ($244.9) million debt restructuring, converting the March 2011 short-term obligations into long-term debt, thereby reducing the district's accumulated deficit to about $83 million, with operating surpluses further decreasing the deficit.[22] The lower net interest rate on the debt will save the district millions in debt-servicing costs. Then, in May 2012, the district took advantage of favorable municipal bond market interest rate conditions. It restructured its long-term debt, through a $141 million refinancing, further reducing its interest expenses.[23]

Although projections estimate eliminating the district's accumulated deficit by 2016, in total the DPS system now has in excess of $2 billion in debt obligations, from four bond sales—including one in 2011, a $245 million debt restructuring, and another in 2012, a $141 million refinancing. It also has outstanding $2 billion in bonds voters approved, $1.5 billion in 1994 and $500 million in 2009, for facilities improvements, which comprise the district's Capital Project Funds.

Similar to the city, the DPS district ought to accelerate the reduction of the principal amount of these obligations, particularly those that bear interest. With its financial viability hopefully achieved, particularly with the enactment of the 2012 Local Financial Stability and Choice Act, the DPS district may generate sufficient surpluses to implement an enhanced debt reduction plan. Apart from the will to unburden future generations from past spending excesses on facilities, future enrollment drops—including competition for students from charter schools and schools in inner-ring suburbs, which will result in declining revenues—this represents a challenge to the district's ability to pay off its massive long-term debt ahead of schedule.

Funding Facilities' Improvements

In November 2009, Detroit voters approved a $500 million bond issue (Proposal S) to fund the construction of eight new school buildings, the renovation of ten existing ones, and the demolition of one old high school.[24] The new and renovated schools will include more levels at each facility. By combining resources, the new and renovated buildings will further reduce the district's overall operating costs.

Under Proposal S, the DPS system borrowed some $500 million through the 2009 federal stimulus program (the American Recovery and Reinvestment Act of 2009), specifically, $246 million in Qualified School Construction Bonds, a fifteen-year loan to be repaid at zero interest, and $254 million in Build America Bonds, which provide for a 35 percent reduction in the effective interest rate, with the interest rate based on Michigan's school bond loan program. The funds could only be used for new building construction, remodeling buildings, furnishing and equipping schools, not for teacher or administrator salaries, operating expenses, or routine repairs.

To prevent the mishandling of the borrowed funds, an oversight committee, the DPS Bond Advisory and Fiscal Responsibility Committee, was created. The committee, consisting of community leaders, parents, business leaders, and political officials, ensured accountability. It supervised the construction process and saw that the objectives of the facilities renewal plan were met on time and within budget.

Detroit Public School District's Strategic Plan

Proposal S represented part of a larger school construction and renovation program, the Detroit Public Schools Master Facilities Plan.[25] As formulated under Bobb's leadership, the five-year plan, which covers the period 2010–15, identified five priorities: academic rebirth; facility renewal; fiscal responsibility; a neighborhood focus; and safety and security. The plan reimagines the entire school district. It eliminates middle schools in favor of a pre-K–8 model to limit the need for students to transition to a new school. The plan also creates new pre-K–12 schools and some pre-K–14 campuses. It includes nonacademic facilities, such as swimming pools and recreation centers in the new schools, designed to make these buildings the center of a community. By creating multi-level school campuses and open-use sports complexes, the plan will not only reinvigorate schools but also hopefully contribute to neighborhood redevelopment.

Under the facilities construction and renovation plan, Detroit residents would see no tax increases. On completion, some 75 percent of DPS students will attend new or recently renovated schools.

Education Achievement System: A Statewide Plan

With DPS district's facilities taken care of, in June 2011, Roberts and Governor Snyder jointly unveiled a statewide, long-range school overhaul plan.[26] The plan calls for placing the lowest performing 5 percent of all Michigan schools, so-called distressed schools, under a new statewide school system, the Education Achievement System (EAS). As proposed, the EAS would put millions of additional dollars into the classroom, by squeezing and streamlining a local district's central office bureaucracy in favor of classroom teachers. Instead of the DPS system, for example, spending 55 percent of its funds at the classroom level, with the rest allocated to administration, debt service, and maintenance—under the plan, initially 67 percent and ultimately 95 percent of each school's funds will flow to the classroom. The combined EAS and local district organizations will be smaller than those of the existing districts, hopefully allowing more dollars to be spent in the classroom.

Although a district's per-student funding allocations will remain the same, driving considerably more funds into the classroom will, proponents expect, lead to smaller class sizes; more student-teacher contact; and a better chance for teachers to evaluate and help each student—thereby contributing to heightened academic achievement. Under a continuous improvement model, teachers will constantly monitor each student to ascertain if he or she is falling behind and re-teach content according to individual needs and assess progress. As students master subject matter at one level, they proceed to the next level, with advancement based on the mastery of materials, not the number of days spent in class. Students requiring extra time to complete material will not start over at the beginning of a new school year, but will work from their past achievement levels. In addition to providing more individualized instruction, EAS schools will increase the number of days students are in the classroom from 170 to 210 and implement an eight-hour school day. An extended school year and school day will give teachers more time to bring students up to and above grade level. In sum, through EAS, Snyder and Roberts sought to raise academic achievement in "failing" schools and help more students attain academic success.

EAS schools will also increase the autonomy of and flexibility for principals. Each principal received the nearly ultimate power for running his or her EAS school, including hiring, placing, training, supporting, and firing teachers, and, more generally, spending resources, to provide continuous improvement based on each student's needs.

The Educational Achievement Authority (EAA), an independent, free-standing public entity, governs the EAS. The DPS system, Eastern Michigan University (EMU), and the Michigan governor appoint the eleven-member board, with two members appointed by the DPS district, two by EMU, and seven by the governor.

With respect to the DPS system, in the fall of 2012, the EAS took over fifteen low-performing DPSs, six high schools as well as nine elementary and middle schools, with about 10,000 students.[27] Based on the age and condition of buildings as well as student population and achievement levels, these schools were removed from the district and placed under the EAS. Families were given the choice to transfer their children to a different school or enroll them in their same school now under the EAS. Students from other schools could enroll in EAS schools in Detroit.

Although all the fifteen EAS schools' physical facilities were placed under EAA's control, they remain the DPS district's property, with the EAA responsible for building maintenance and repairs. After five years, if a school makes adequate progress it could return to the DPS system, remain in the EAS, or become an independently run charter school.

Granting Quasi-Charter School Status

As a further step to empowering Detroit's public schools, making them more entrepreneurial and innovative, effective in the fall of 2012, Roberts gave nine theme-based high schools quasi-charter status.[28] The plan represented a transition to site-based management, a system of schools, not a single, large, bureaucratic entity run from the top down. At each of these self-governing schools, choices about hiring, curriculum, and budget are made at the school level. In making decisions to best serve the needs of their particular students, if a school wishes to retain its self-governing rights and status, it must set and meet academic and financial goals. In concept, principals serve as instructional leaders, not chief administrative officers. Principals and teachers in these schools are expected to take advantage of the enhanced autonomy and flexibility at the school level to pursue learning strategies that work. Each school has a governing council—consisting of civic, community, business, government, and local leaders, together with parents—that takes responsibility for the school's performance in partnership with its principal and teachers. Each council controls a school's budget, hiring, curriculum, and operations, under the DPS system's oversight, to best meet student needs. The DPS district hoped to place 97 percent of state funds at each quasi-charter school's level, after deducting debt service and fixed-cost obligations, as well as 100 percent of available federal funds.

In addition to the nine small high schools, with a projected enrollment of 2,800 students, the Office of Self-Governing Schools also manages sixteen DPS-authorized charters, for a total of twenty-five self-governing schools. The district continues to be responsible for its eighty-nine centrally supported schools.

Some Broader Educational Policy Questions

Stepping back from the whirlwind of activity from 2009–12, the DPS district must significantly improve the academic performance of its schools, and raise its high school graduation rate, while providing rigorous standards and interventions for low-performing students. Recognizing that not everyone is capable of or should pursue a four-year (or even a two-year) college degree, it is time to rehabilitate vocational (career and technical) education in Detroit high schools to prepare graduates for the new labor markets, including tech and health care jobs, among others. High schools ought to form partnerships with local businesses to train students for meaningful careers in growing fields. Furthermore, by keeping them motivated, more students will graduate from high school with marketable skills.[29]

More generally, students from poverty-stricken families present a number of education challenges: poor attendance, nutrition, and health adversely impact in-class performance; high transiency disrupts learning patterns at home and in school; and fewer models of success surround these students. They find it more difficult to concentrate, to sit still, to follow directions, and to rebound from disappointments.

However, a good education, one focused on turning these omnipresent challenges into character-building successes, provides the best route out of poverty. One possible model, the Harlem Children's Zone, takes a holistic approach, combining education and a conveyor belt of various expensive social services. Another approach, Turnaround for Children,[30] is far less expensive. In brief, a three-person Turnaround team works with a school for three to five years. One person assists the principal in creating a positive culture, where students believe they can succeed. Another works with teachers to minimize disruptions in the classroom. While a third, a social worker, trains school personnel to deal with the emotional and psychological needs of children from low-income families, identifying the most troubled students and contracting with outside mental health organizations to provide services to these students.

Even apart from these approaches, K–12 public schools in Detroit, whether public or charter, must, at least, provide high expectations for students, helping them start believing in themselves and that they can do the work. Parental participation and involvement in their children's education is critical. K–12 schools must also emphasize character education, both moral and performance, including self-discipline, resilience, responsibility for one's self and one's community, hope for the future, and a work ethic, to bolster one's chances of advancing economically and achieving a happy, meaningful, productive life.[31] To enhance academic achievement and foster character education, the DPS district may need the conversion of all its remaining schools to charter or quasi-charter status.[32] Even assuming a vast improvement in students' skills and improved high school graduation rates, profit-oriented, innovative Detroit-area businesses, big and small, as analyzed in the next chapter, will not be able to absorb everyone. Students, as they graduate from high school, must further their education, look for jobs outside the region, or turn to entrepreneurship to create their own opportunities. To meet this challenge, the DPS district could offer entrepreneurial-oriented courses in its public high schools, integrating technology and entrepreneurship in all classes,[33] combined with industry partnerships, perhaps even creating a charter high school for entrepreneurship. However, entrepreneurship may not be high on the agenda of the teachers' union.

Beyond bringing fiscal sanity and sustainability to Detroit and the DPS District as well as attempting to concentrate public services in denser, more stable neighborhoods, Detroit faces a need for an invigorated for-profit private sector, including large firms and start-ups, to create jobs and enhance its tax base.

Notes

1. For a history of the Detroit Public School District, focusing on funding, see Jeffrey Mirel, *The Rise and Fall of an Urban School System: Detroit, 1907–81* (Ann Arbor: University of Michigan, 1993).
2. The statistics in this paragraph are from US Department of Education, Institute of Education Statistics, The Nation's Report Card (Report Card), Reading 2009, Trial Urban District Assessment, Results at Grades 4 and 8, NCES 2010-459, 50–51; Report Card, Reading 2011, Trial Urban District Assessment, Results at Grades 4 and 8, NCES 2012-455, 76–77. See also

Jennifer Chambers, "Detroit students get mixed results," *Detroit News,* December 8, 2011, A15; Chastity Pratt Dawsey, "DPS students still lagging in reading, math," *Detroit Free Press,* December 8, 2011, A6; Jennifer Chambers, "Sweeping overhaul set for ailing Mich. schools," *Detroit News,* June 21, 2011, A1; Chastity Pratt Dawsey and Lori Higgins, "Scores on test trigger plans to change what DPS teaches," *Detroit Free Press,* May 21, 2010, A4; Chastity Pratt Dawsey and Robin Erb, "Experts: What's missing is a value on education," *Detroit Free Press,* December 9, 2009, A10.

A large-scale analysis of urban trends on the National Assessment of Educational Progress identified six reform strategies to boost math and reading performance: strong leadership; robust accountability mechanisms; a coherent curriculum; professional development programming; district-wide support; and quantitative assessment. Michael Casserly et al., Pieces of the Puzzle: Factors in the Improvement of Urban School Districts on the National Assessment of Educational Progress, Council of the Great City Schools and American Institutes for Research, Fall 2011, and Michael Casserly, Pieces of the Puzzle: Factors in Improving Achievement of Urban School Districts, Education Outlook No. 4, American Enterprise Institute, July 2012.

3. Report Card, Mathematics 2009, Trial Urban District Assessment, Results at Grades 4 and 8, NCES 2010-452, 46–47. See also Jennifer Chambers, "Detroit students get mixed results," *Detroit News,* December 8, 2011, A15.

DPS students achieved even lower scores on the 2009 NAEP science test, with 74 percent of Detroit fourth-graders and 80 percent of its eighth-grade students scoring below basic level science understanding. Report Card, Science 2009, Trial Urban District Assessment, Results at Grades 4 and 8, NCES 2011-452, 52–53. See also Chastity Pratt Dawsey, "DPS science scores worst among 17 cities," *Detroit Free Press,* February 25, 2011, A9.

4. Chastity Pratt Dawsey, Robin Erb, Lori Higgins, "Big ideas for Mich. Schools," *Detroit Free Press,* February 9, 2010, A6.

Poor student attendance also has a financial impact on the cash-strapped DPS system. For example, the DPS District will lose $4.2 million in state aid during the next four years (2012–2016) because student attendance fell below the state mandated 75 percent level on ten days during the 2010–11 school year. Jennifer Chambers, "Poor student attendance costs DPS $4.2M," *Detroit News,* June 12, 2012, A3.

5. Detroit Public Schools (DPS), Press Release, "DPS reaches 62 percent graduation rate, the highest since state began new cohort methodology in 2007," February 22, 2011 <www.Detroitk12.org/content/2011/02/22/dps-reaches-62-percent-graduation-rate> (November 22, 2011).

Excellent Schools Detroit, a coalition of philanthropic leaders (from The Skillman Foundation, The Kresge Foundation, the W.K. Kellogg Foundation, and the McGregor Fund), politicians, and parents has outlined an ambitious vision to put Detroit on the path to be the first major US city by 2020 where 90 percent of its students graduate from high school and 90 percent enroll in college or quality postsecondary training programs. The Skillman Foundation, Press Release, "Coalition pledges multiple actions to prepare Detroit's students for college, careers," March 11, 2010 <www.skillman.org/News-and-Events/Press-Releases/Coalition-pledges-multiple> (December 8, 2011). See also

Chastity Pratt Dawsey and Peggy Walsh-Sarnecki, "College part of plan, too," *Detroit Free Press,* March 11, 2010, A6, and Steven Gray, "Detroit's Class Act," *Fortune* 162:3 (August 16, 2010): 49–50.

6. *Education Week,* "Graduation Policies for the Class of 2007" 26:40 (June 12, 2007): 38–42, at 42, reported the DPS's high school graduation rate at 24.9 percent, the lowest graduation rate among the nation's fifty largest districts.

7. DPS, District Data, April 11, 2001 and DPS, Press Release, "DPS enrolls 66,007 students – 73,306 including charter and Pre-K, exceeds budget projection and turns back five-year enrollment trend," October 20, 2011 <www.detroitk12.org/content/2011/10/20/dps-enrolls-65971-students> (November 22, 2011). See also Jennifer Chambers, "DPS, EAA reach 90% attendance mark, showing gains in enrollment, *Detroit News,* September 20, 2012, A4, and Jennifer Chambers, "DPS plans to cut 1,900 jobs for fall," *Detroit News,* June 21, 2012, A1.

    For enrollment declines in big school districts across the United States see Motoko Rich, "Enrollment Off in Big Districts, Forcing Layoffs," *New York Times,* July 24, 2012, A1.

8. Detroit Public School District Financial Review Team, Report of the Detroit Public School District Financial Review Team, November 6, 2008, and Michigan Department of Education, Press Release, "Detroit Schools in Financial Emergency; Financial Manager to be Appointed," December 8, 2008. See also Chasity Pratt Dawsey and Peggy Walsh-Sarnecki, "At DPS, a State Watchdog May Control More Than Cash," *Detroit Free Press,* December 9, 2008, NWS1.

9. Office of the Governor, Press Release, "Governor Appoints Robert C. Bobb Emergency Financial Manager for Detroit Public Schools," January 26, 2009 <www.michigan.gov> (November 28, 2011). Bobb was appointed under Michigan Public Act 72 of 1990 (Local Government and Fiscal Responsibility Act). His appointment for 2009–2010 was noticed in a message from the Governor to the Michigan Senate, January 27, 2009. State of Michigan, Journal of the Senate, 95th Legislature, Regular Session of 2009, No. 3, January 28, 2009, 32. See also Chasity Pratt Dawsey, "Detroit schools get financial manager," *Detroit Free Press,* January 27, 2009, NWS3, and Jennifer Mrozowski, "New manager takes on DPS," *Detroit News,* January 27, 2009, A3.

10. For Bobb's achievements as emergency financial manager see generally Nick Anderson, "Why D.C. keeps an eye on Detroit school leader," *Washington Post,* December 25, 2010, A1. See also Chastity Pratt Dawsey, "Excess spending found under Bobb," *Detroit Free Press,* June 24, 2011, A5; Lori Higgins and Chastity Pratt Dawsey, "Bobb warns teachers," *Detroit Free Press,* April 15, 2011, A1; Marisa Schultz, "DPS board will review academic programs," *Detroit News,* December 8, 2010, A1; Rochelle Riley, "Bobb will depart DPS with pride, regrets," *Detroit Free Press,* October 23, 2010, A2; Peggy Walsh–Sarnecki, "Bulking up on reading, math," *Detroit Free Press,* July 21, 2010, A3; Chastity Pratt Dawsey, "Hopes high summer school can boost DPS," *Detroit Free Press,* May 8, 2010, A9; Marisa Schultz, "DPS deficit grows under Bob," *Detroit News,* March 10, 2010, A1; Dakara I. Aarons, "Decline and Fall," *Education Week* 28:37 (August 12, 2009): 24–27.

11. Bobb engaged in a long legal battle with the Detroit school board from August 2009 to March 2011 with respect to his ability to implement various

academic changes. With the March 2011 enactment of a revised emergency manager act (Public Act 4 of 2011 [Local Government and School District Fiscal Accountability Act]) that gave Bobb authority to make all financial and academic decisions, Wayne County Circuit Judge Wendy Baxter gave academic control of the DPS District to Bobb. See Chastity Pratt Dawsey, "New law puts Bobb in full control of DPS, judge agrees," *Detroit Free Press,* March 19, 2011, A3, and Doug Guthrie and Jennifer Chambers, "Bobb gains control of academics," *Detroit News,* March 19, 2011, A1.

Previously, in April 2010, Judge Baxter had granted the school board a preliminary injunction to halt Bobb's authority over academic matters that was reversed on appeal. Adams v. Bobb, Case No. 09-020160 AW (Mich. Circuit Ct. April 16, 2010). In December 2010, Judge Baxter granted the school a permanent injunction. Adams v. Bobb, Case No. 09-020160 AW (Mich. Circuit Ct. December 6, 2010). See also Jennifer Chambers, "No academic role for Bobb," *Detroit News,* February 12, 2011, A4; Marisa Schultz, "Lawmakers urge Bobb not to appeal," *Detroit News,* December 10, 2010, A1; Chasity Pratt Dawsey and Lori Higgins, "Judge: Bobb went too far," *Detroit Free Press,* December 7, 2010, A1; Marisa Schultz, "Judge: Bobb exceeded power on academics," *Detroit News,* December 7, 2010, A1; Lori Higgins, "Bobb's supporters praise ruling, but others see sad day for district," *Detroit Free Press,* May 7, 2010, A16; Chastity Pratt Dawsey, "Court backs Bobb," *Detroit Free Press,* May 7, 2010, A1; Chastity Pratt Dawsey, "Fight over future of DPS isn't over yet, board plans to seek injunction," *Detroit Free Press,* May 7, 2010, A16; Chastity Pratt Dawsey, "Cox files appeal to reverse injunction against Bobb," *Detroit Free Press,* April 24, 2010, A3; Chastity Pratt Dawsey and Lori Higgins, "Judge is firm on her DPS ruling," *Detroit Free Press,* April 22, 2010, A9; Chastity Pratt Dawsey, "Ruling doesn't mean Bobb must do what board wants," *Detroit Free Press,* April 17, 2010, A4; Marisa Schultz, "School board sues Bobb," *Detroit News,* August 18, 2009, A5.

12. School District of the City of Detroit, Settlement Proposal to the Detroit Federation of Teachers, Local 231, December 9, 2009.

13. Michael Winerip, "For Detroit Schools, Hope for the Hopeless," *New York Times,* March 14, 2011, A13.

14. DPS, Press Release, "Detroit Public Schools completes $231 million short-term cash flow financing, ensuring district will make payroll, meet obligations," March 3, 2011 <detroitk12.org/content/2011/03/03/detroit-public-schools-completes-231-million> (November 29, 2011).

15. For background on Roberts see Jennifer Chambers, "From poverty to privilege through learning," *Detroit News,* July 27, 2011, A1.

16. Contract for Emergency Manager Services, Rick Snyder, Governor and Roy Roberts, Emergency Manager, May 4, 2011; Office of the Governor, Rick Snyder, Press Release, "Snyder appoints Roy S. Roberts Detroit Public Schools emergency manager," May 4, 2011; Roy S. Roberts, Order Announcing Roy S. Roberts as the Emergency Manager for the School District of the City of Detroit Effective May 16, 2011, June 9, 2011, Order 2011-EMRR1. Roberts was appointed under Michigan Public Act 4 of 2011 (Local Government and School District Fiscal Accountability Act), which gave emergency managers new powers, including the ability to amend or abrogate union contracts. See also Jennifer Chambers and Leonard N. Fleming,

"Ex-GM exec to control DPS," *Detroit News,* May 5, 2011, A1, and Chastity Pratt Dawsey, "Ex-GM exec to lead schools," *Detroit Free Press,* May 5, 2011, A1. Public Act 4 was suspended from August 8, 2012 until November 6, 2012. During this chaotic period, and subsequently as the result of Michigan voters repealing Public Act 4 in November 2012, the Detroit School Board regained authority over academics in DPS District, with Roberts having authority over finances under the 1990 emergency financial manager law. Any academic decisions having financial implications requiring Roberts' approval. See Jennifer Chambers, "Court Upholds Appointment," *Detroit News,* November 17, 2012, A3. With the enactment of the 2012 Local Financial Stability and Choice Act, Roberts regained authority over academic matters in March 2013.

17.   Jennifer Chambers, "Class sizes may grow in DPS," *Detroit News,* July 13, 2012, A4.

18.   Jennifer Chambers, "DPS students targeted for summer," *Detroit News,* May 30, 2012, A4.

19.   Chastity Pratt Dawsey, "Roberts OKs 10% pay cut at DPS," *Detroit Free Press,* July 30, 2011, A1; Chastity Pratt Dawsey and Lori Higgins, "As DPS cut, it spent big on trips and consultants," *Detroit Free Press,* June 24, 2011, A1; Jennifer Chambers, "DPS wages, jobs to be slashed," *Detroit News,* June 24, 2011, A1.

20.   Kim Kozlowski, "DPS reveals new contract details online," *Detroit News,* July 7, 2012, A3. See also Shawn D. Lewis, "Union balks at imposed DPS contract," *Detroit News,* July 3, 2012, A1, and Chastity Pratt Dawsey, "Union: DPS pact to cut teacher benefits," *Detroit Free Press,* July 3, 2012, A3.

In August 2012, Roberts announced a bonus of up to 5 percent to all employees if the district meets financial targets. For each $5 million of general operating surplus the district has at the end of its 2011–12 and 2012–13 fiscal years, each eligible employee will receive a 1 percent wage bonus of his or her base annual salary. Jennifer Chambers, "Roberts give DPS staffers bonuses," *Detroit News,* September 1, 2012, A1, and Chastity Pratt Dawsey, "DPS workers to get 2% bonus after expected budget surplus," *Detroit Free Press,* September 1, 2012 <LexisNexis>. Employees received a one-time bonus equal to 2 percent of base salary in December 2012. Jennifer Chambers, "DPS employees to get bonus," *Detroit News,* December 12, 2012, A4.

21.   DPS, Emergency Manager, Fiscal Year 2013, Proposed Budgets, n.d., 24 (DPS, FY2013, Proposed Budget, General Fund). See also Mark Hicks, "DPS parents raise concerns over budget," *Detroit News,* June 28, 2012, A6, and Chastity Pratt Dawsey, "DPS gamble: Cuts improve district," *Detroit Free Press,* June 28, 2012, A6; Chambers, "DPS plans;" Chastity Pratt Dawsey, "Shrinking DPS will cut 1,889 more jobs," *Detroit Free Press,* June 21, 2012, A1.

22.   DPS, Press Release, "DPS completes $244.9 million financing after receiving 'A+' credit rating, completing a key element in district's financial turnaround plan," October 7, 2011 <www.detroitk12.org/content/2011/10/07> (June 21, 2012). See also Jennifer Chambers, "DPS refinancing $245M of debt to ease its deficit," *Detroit News,* October 8, 2011, A4.

23.   DPS, Press Release, "DPS Completes Restructure of 2005 Debt and Saves District over $8 million in Interest Costs," May 10, 2012 and DPS, Emergency Manager, Fiscal Year 2013, Proposed Budgets, n.d., 21–22.

24. Robert Bobb, Press Release, "A thank you from Robert Bobb," November 6, 2009 <www.detroit12.org/proposal_s> (November 29, 2011) and Marisa Schultz, "DPS seeks $500M bond," *Detroit News,* August 26, 2009, A3.
25. Office of the Emergency Financial Manager, Detroit Public Schools Master Facilities Plan 2010–2015, March 17, 2010. After extensive community input, the master facilities plan underwent changes, specifically, with respect to school closures. DPS, Press Release, "Detroit Public Schools Master Facilities Plan undergoes significant changes following input from community, June 7, 2010 <www.detroitk12.org/content/2010/06/07> (June 21, 2012). See also Chastity Pratt Dawsey, "A peek at DPS's new look," *Detroit Free Press,* August 17, 2011, A1; Robin Erb, "What DPS wants to improve," *Detroit Free Press,* March 15, 2010, A9; Marty Weil, "Transforming Detroit," *Scholastic Administr@tor:* Back to School Supplement 10:1 (2010): 37–38, at 40.
26. Office of the Governor, Press Release, "Governor, Detroit Public Schools Emergency Manager jointly unveil dramatic education reform plan to restructure failing Michigan schools," June 20, 2011 <www.michigan.gov> (November 22, 2011), and Education Achievement System, "Frequently Asked Questions" <www.michigan.gov/printerfriendly/0,1687,7-281-59278---,00.html> (June 12, 2012). See also Jennifer Chambers, "Sweeping overhaul set for ailing Mich. Schools," *Detroit News,* June 21, 2011, A1; Chastity Pratt Dawsey, "New start for worst schools," *Detroit Free Press,* June 21, 2011, A1; David Jess, Chastity Pratt Dawsey, Chris Christoff, "Failing schools won't be in DPS," *Detroit Free Press,* June 20, 2011, A1.
27. Education Achievement Authority of Michigan, Press Release, "Education Achievement Authority of Michigan announces start-up schools," March 13, 2012 <www.detroitk12.org/content/2012/03/13/education-achievement-authority-of-michigan> (June 7, 2012). See also Jennifer Chambers and Shawn D. Lewis, "State to take over 15 DPS schools," *Detroit News,* March 14, 2012, A3, and Chastity Pratt Dawsey, "State names Detroit schools for takeover," *Detroit Free Press,* March 14, 2012, A3. At the fifteen schools, the EAA outsourced eleven services, including custodial and maintenance services, to private contractors. Chastity Pratt Dawsey, "DPS union leadership criticizes new EAA," *Detroit Free Press,* June 30, 2012, A4.

With the repeal of the 2011 emergency manager act, the Detroit school board voted to withdraw from the EAA agreement and demanded that the fifteen schools be transferred back to the DPS. Chastity Pratt Dawsey, "Bills could change the way struggling schools run," *Detroit Free Press,* November 24, 2012, A1.

During the suspension of the 2011 emergency manager law, the Board of Education sought to cancel the transfer of the fifteen schools to the EAA. However, the board's decision was subject to corroboration by Roberts, who did not recognize the decision and it did not take effect. Chastity Pratt Dawsey, "DPS board OKs subpoena of Roberts to answer questions," *Detroit Free Press,* August 28, 2012 <LexisNexis>. The board previously had lost a lawsuit to regain control of the fifteen schools transferred to the EAA. Jennifer Chambers, "Judge: 15 failing DPS schools must stay in EAA," *Detroit News,* August 15, 2012, A1, and Chastity Pratt Dawsey, "Wayne County judge gives board control over DPS academics," *Detroit Free Press,* August 15, 2012 <LexisNexis>.

28. DPS Emergency Manager, Press Release, "DPS Emergency Manager Roy Roberts announces 2012–2013 Action Plans: Increasing Quality Seats for Detroit School Children," April 5, 2012 <www.detroitk12.org/content/2012/04/05/dps-emergency-manager-roy-roberts-announces> (June 7, 2012). See also Jennifer Chambers, "DPS proposes 10 self-governing schools," *Detroit News,* April 5, 2012, A1, and Chastity Pratt Dawsey, "Leaders to aid self-run DPS schools," *Detroit Free Press,* June 5, 2012, A3.

29. Lewis D. Solomon, *Cycles of Poverty and Crime in America's Inner Cities* (New Brunswick, N.J., 2012), 109–129, 146–150.

30. Joe Nocera, "Addressing Poverty in Schools," *New York Times,* July 28, 2012, A17.

31. For an analysis of the character hypothesis, namely, that noncognitive skills, such as persistence, self-control, curiosity, conscientiousness, and self-confidence, are more crucial to achieving success than cognitive skills, see Paul Tough, *How Children Succeed: Grit, Curiosity, and the Hidden Power of Character* (Boston: Houghton Mifflin Harcourt, 2012).

32. Highland Park, Michigan, public school district, one of Michigan's lowest performing academically, turned its three schools over to a for-profit charter school company. See Stephanie Banchero and Matthew Dolan, "Michigan City Outsources All of Its Schools," *Wall Street Journal,* August 8, 2012, A3.

   For an optimistic view of the impact of charter schools on students' academic performance, see Matthew Kaminski, "Weekend Interview with John White," *Wall Street Journal,* October 8–9, 2011, A13, but see Trip Gabriel, "Many Charter Schools, Varied Grades," *New York Times,* May 2, 2010, 1, and Michael Winerip, "For Detroit Schools, Hope for the Hopeless," *New York Times,* March 14, 2011, A1.

   For an analysis of various education policies to improve the learning outcomes of children from low-income families, see, e.g., Brian Jacobs and Jens Ludwig, Improving Educational Outcomes for Poor Children, National Bureau of Economic Research, Working Paper 14550, December 2008. See also Diane Ravitch, "School 'Reform': A Failing Grade," *New York Review of Books,* September 29, 2011, 32–35.

33. J. J. Colao, "Teaching Success," *Forbes* 189:9 (May 21, 2012): 46–48.

III

Economic Growth
and Job Creation Fueled
by the Private Sector

In the intermediate and long term, a resurgent, more diversified, for-profit private sector, along with foundations and other nonprofit organizations, will help propel Detroit's economic growth and job creation. An unofficial coalition of business and foundation interests—led by Dan Gilbert, founder and chairman of Quicken Loans, and Rip Rapson of The Kresge Foundation, as well as various nonprofit organizations, including medical centers and higher education institutions—are investing millions in Detroit, particularly in the downtown and the Midtown areas. Realizing that future economic development will come from the private sector, not public-sector spending, they share a blueprint for urban revitalization known as "place making." Simply put, metropolitan areas anchored by vibrant central cities and their cores, serve as talent magnets. These talent magnets, in combination with sound tax regulatory fundamentals, drive prosperity. As jobs and income grow, so will Detroit's tax revenues, enabling it to provide quality public services.

This part of the book contains two chapters. Chapter 6 examines the impact of corporate relocations into the city. Although rebuilding Detroit's tax base and helping its retail sector, these moves will not significantly reduce Detroit's unemployment rate. Most businesses transferred existing workers from the suburbs. Also considered are financial repopulation incentives provided by businesses, nonprofit organizations, and foundations. For all the excitement about in-town living, it is uncertain whether downtown and surrounding areas will develop sufficient density. Currently, the demand appears to exceed the available supply of housing options. The coming of a Whole Foods store to Midtown, however, points to one firm's bet on the vitality of a new urban core in Detroit. Finally, the chapter reaffirms the need for collaboration through public-private partnerships as a significant economic development vehicle. However, a business-foundation group's most notable public-private partnership, the M-1 Light Rail, failed to come to fruition.

Chapter 7 discusses the role of entrepreneurs, who build companies and employ people, in Detroit's revitalization. The chapter examines the city's need to encourage start-up and small-business growth. Also considered is the possible role of the Creative Class in facilitating economic growth. It concludes that the Creative Class seems destined to play a more limited role than entrepreneurs, more generally, in promoting economic development and job creation.

Detroit's human capital challenge represents a significant obstacle to revitalization, and underpins the analysis in chapters 6 and 7. The mismatch between new jobs—whether created by big corporations or small businesses, now and likely in the future—and adult residents' skills and education levels, appears nearly insurmountable, even if the public sector, foundations, and wealthy individuals pour additional resources into job training.

6

Economic Development through Corporate Relocations, Financial Repopulation Incentives, and Public-Private Partnerships

The last few years have witnessed two significant developments: corporate relocations, especially by high-tech firms, into downtown Detroit and the use of financial incentives to encourage repopulation. The corporate moves will probably help retailers along a key section of Woodward Avenue, assist selected areas of the residential market, and raise revenues from the commuter tax on nonresidents who work in Detroit. However, the relocations did not significantly impact on the city's joblessness, because most businesses brought existing workers in from the suburbs. If the repopulation incentives generate sufficient density, visions of downtown and certain other areas as the lively core of a revitalized city may come to fruition. Whole Foods's opening of a store in Midtown represents an encouraging trend.

The chapter also stresses the need for more collaboration between the public and private sectors, particularly in the form of public-private partnerships. Although the M-1 Light Rail public-private partnership did not come to fruition, it marked a notable, hopeful attempted effort in Detroit's revitalization. With the creation of a regional transit authority, approved by the Michigan legislature in December 2012, improved access by city residents to public transit hopefully will help overcome the spatial mismatch between the location of jobs and people and help reduce, to some degree, joblessness.

Corporate Relocations into Downtown Detroit

In the first decade of the twenty-first century, corporations began to relocate their offices into Detroit's downtown central business district from the suburbs. Information technology companies, including Compuware Corp., Quicken Loans, Inc., and GalexE. Solutions, Inc., have clustered in the city. This small concentration of high-technology firms will hopefully draw more tech businesses into downtown. Corporate relocations were, however, not limited to high-tech companies.

High-Tech Firms. The cluster of high-tech firms began to take shape when Compuware Corp., a software publisher, moved its headquarters from the suburbs to downtown in 2003.[1] Peter Karmanos Jr., co-founder, CEO, and chairman of Compuware, sparked the trend, when the firm relocated into its new world headquarters building, overlooking Campus Martius Park. Located in the downtown central business district, a mix of donors, corporate, individual, and foundations, including Skillman, Hudson-Webber, Kresge, McGregor, and the Community Foundation of Southeast Michigan, funded the park's construction in 2003 at the cost of $20 million. After 2003, the emerging technology hub happened partly by serendipity and partly by plan. As Karmanos stated, "If conditions are right and there's enough synergy, and you start to build a critical mass by hook or by crook, I think we'll see another sizable software company move around here."[2] That event, however, took time.

Quicken Loans's arrival in 2010 added to the momentum, followed by a small technology firm, GalexE. Solutions. These corporate relocations helped begin downtown's redefinition from mainly a home to banks, law firms, and government employees to more of an emerging technologies and service industry-oriented flavor, after the influx of Quicken's Internet-based team and then the Blue Cross health care insurance workers.

The nation's largest online retail mortgage lender, Quicken Loans, and its sister companies, moved their headquarters and initially about 1,700 employees from suburban Livonia, Michigan, to Detroit in August 2010.[3] The firm leased nearly 250,000 square feet of space for five years in the Compuware Building. In October 2011, Quicken shifted another 1,500 workers to the Chase Tower Building, with 1,000 more to the First National Bank Building the next month.[4] Gilbert and his real estate partners, through Rock Ventures LLC, had previously acquired both of these buildings earlier in 2011. Quicken also announced plans to begin construction in mid-2013 of its own world headquarters building on Woodward Avenue, Detroit's historic commercial spine. Then, in July 2012, a Rock Ventures unit, Title Source, transferred 500 employees to the First National Bank Building with another 1,000 workers coming during the next six months.[5] The move enabled Title Source to consolidate employees from offices in suburban Troy and Farmington Hills. By early 2013, some 6,000 workers from Gilbert-affiliated firms had moved to downtown Detroit.

In moving Quicken's headquarters to downtown, Gilbert wanted to make a statement and attract other high-tech businesses to Woodward Avenue, what he likes to call "Webward Avenue,"[6] Detroit's emerging technology district. Reflecting Gilbert's technology spin, he hopes for a hive of high-tech firms with employees eating, working, and living in downtown, buzzing with innovative ideas for the future of Detroit's new knowledge-based, brain-driven economy. Gilbert wants to make downtown the lively core of a revitalized city, what he calls Detroit 2.0, rich with high-tech entrepreneurial activity and a bustling new economy. However, Gilbert's relocation decision was not entirely altruistic. For example, in making the move, Quicken received some $47 ($47.2) million in state tax credits from the Michigan Economic Growth Authority.[7]

Beyond his employee relocation plans, Gilbert sought to own enough real estate to attract other companies to downtown, thereby implementing his vision of making Detroit an Internet and digital-technology hub. Gilbert also thought that 2011 represented a buy-low time. He felt the city was going to turn around and wanted to be on the ground floor from an investment standpoint. Believing that property prices had nowhere to go but up, Gilbert scooped up downtown office buildings at bargain prices, even by Detroit's depressed standards.

In quick succession in 2011–12, through Rock Ventures LLC, Gilbert acquired nine buildings at steep discounts.[8] Notably, in April 2011, he acquired the Chase Tower, a fourteen-story building one-third (34.8%) empty, designed by the noted architect Alfred Kahn. Then in August, Rock Ventures paid $8.1 million for the half-empty 800,000-square-foot, twenty-five-story First National Bank Building, also designed by Kahn. At $10 per square foot, the price was near the ten-year low of $9 a square foot touched in 2005 for large Detroit office buildings. In 2011, Gilbert also acquired: the small five-story Madison Theatre Building, which was turned into an entrepreneurial base for high-tech and creative start-up companies; the twenty-three-story Daniel Burnham-designed Dime Building; the six-story Wright-Kay Building at 1500 Woodward Avenue to go with the Lane Bryant Building (1520 Woodward Avenue); the Arts League of Michigan Building (1528 Woodward Avenue); and the 1550 Woodward Building—and the historic Federal Reserve Building, built in 1927, as well as several garages and parking lots.

Smaller moves by companies involved in web-based enterprises also took place. For example, GalexE. Solutions—a New Jersey-based, privately held information technology company, specializing in database management and custom software solutions for health care and retail operations—leased two floors in an almost vacant twenty-five-story office building at 1001 Woodward Avenue.[9] In 2010, it initially moved some 20 employees into the Detroit site and planned to hire an additional 500 workers during the next five years.

A number of factors entered into this firm's decision making. The proximity to the Compuware headquarters and the move by Quicken Loans served as a draw. These were coupled with state tax credits, an inexpensive rent at between $14 and $17 per square foot, rock bottom for a major city, and a gritty, urban ambiance that appeals to young professionals. The firm also sought out a Detroit location because people there would work for lower pay than in other parts of the United States. Although half of the company's worldwide staff is located in India, the firm focused on hiring in the United States as part of its effort to put Americans back to work, while solving time-zone and international political-economy issues.

Non-Tech Firms. Non-tech firms, notably Blue Cross Blue Shield of Michigan (BCBSM) and DTE Energy, also moved employees into downtown Detroit. Beginning in early 2011 and completed by mid-2012, BCBSM transferred 3,400 workers from suburban Southfield, to downtown,[10] to join nearly 3,000 workers already there. With 6,000 employees working downtown, BCBSM became the largest private employer in the city's central business district. Its workers occupy Towers 500 and 600 of the Renaissance Center, a self-contained 1970s complex, whose towers dominate the Detroit riverfront skyline.[11] BCBSM will populate twenty-one floors of Tower 500, with the building's occupancy going from vacant to full, and floors three to ten in Tower 600. In total, it will occupy 435,000 square feet of space in the two buildings for at least fifteen years.

Through the move, BCBSM will save some $30 to $40 million in real estate costs during the fifteen-year period. The relocation eliminated most of the redundancies of operating two separate campuses by creating a single health care insurance workforce, thereby improving operational efficiencies and flexibility. The Blue Cross Network, its health care maintenance organization, remained in Southfield, with about 1,000 employees.

In 2009, the public sector convinced General Motors, which had relocated its headquarters to the Renaissance Center in the 1990s, to stay there rather than move workers to suburban Warren—in part, by providing some $35 million in tax incentives put together by the city, Wayne County, and the state. BCBSM will obtain some of these tax incentives.

In 2011, DTE Energy shifted about 300 workers from its suburban Southfield-based customer service call center to two floors of DTE's downtown headquarters. The company made the move to achieve greater business efficiencies.[12] Then in March 2012, General Motors announced it planned to consolidate its advertising for Chevrolet into a new agency and employ 280 workers downtown.[13]

In May 2012, the Chrysler Group LLC announced that up to seventy executives and employees would get a downtown office in Gilbert's Dime Building, which was renamed the Chrysler House.[14] The move from suburban Auburn Hills marked Chrysler's first presence in downtown Detroit.

Estimates indicate that corporations relocated at least 9,700 workers from the suburbs to downtown from mid-2010 to mid-2012.[15] At present, it is unclear whether these corporate migrations will come to a trickle or more announcements will continue to be forthcoming. In any event, the existing moves will help boost retailers in a key section of Woodward Avenue, the city's signature street, leading commercial real estate analysts to conclude that a retail recovery may be within grasp.[16] Although numerous empty storefronts and empty buildings remain, the hallmarks of economic dysfunctionality, the eight-block stretch of Woodward Avenue between Jefferson Avenue and Grand Circus Park will likely witness increased street-level retail activity, not just during the workweek lunchtime. The corporation migrations will also aid the downtown residential market that took a nosedive in the Great Recession's housing crash. Because Detroit imposes a commuter tax on nonresident workers, the shifts will also help the city's tax base. However, because the relocating firms brought their own workforces from the suburbs, the moves to downtown by tech and non-tech businesses had only a minimal impact on Detroit's unemployment rate.

Also, it is doubtful that the downtown business renaissance will spread outward into the neighborhoods.

Repopulating Detroit

Although Detroit suffered a 25 percent population drop from 2000 to 2010, as noted in chapter 1, some portions of the city experienced repopulation. The area within three miles of downtown saw a 59 percent gain in the number of college-educated residents under age thirty-five from 2000 to 2010. This surge was nearly 30 percent more than two-thirds of the nation's fifty-one largest cities.[17] An increase in young professionals in five areas, Midtown, Woodbridge, New Center, Corktown, and parts of downtown, helped drive the population rise, notably fueled by some 3,200 new residents (17,000 to 20,200) in Midtown from 2000 to 2010.[18]

Immigrants also played a part not only in shifting Detroit's demographics but also in partially stemming the outflow of people.[19] For example, southwest Detroit went from an area that sent workers to auto plants to the center of a thriving Latino community. In addition to counterbalancing population losses to a limited extent, immigrants fuel business creation.[20]

The Importance of Midtown

Only in about 2000, did a twelve-block area begin to be called Midtown. Today, it is becoming the place where empty nesters, ex-suburbanites, young professionals, and out-of-town transplants, who want an urban lifestyle, choose to live, work, and shop.[21] It is a safe, stable area with major museums (the Detroit Institute of Arts and the Charles H. Wright Museum of African American History, among nine museums), various performing arts venues (Max M. Fisher Music Center, the home of the Detroit Symphony Orchestra, the Detroit Opera House, and the nation's second-largest theater district with ten theaters), and an assortment of bars and restaurants, all within walking distance of each other. It is home to higher education institutions, including Wayne State University, the College for Creative Studies, the College of Osteopathic Medicine, the Community Music School of Michigan State University, and the University of Michigan-Detroit Center at Orchestra Place. Midtown has become a destination for entrepreneurs and artists because of the numerous independent (non-chain) stores that have opened since 2005. These ventures include trendy clothing boutiques, gift stores, food-related businesses, and a strong group of some dozen galleries.

Solidifying Midtown's reputation as Detroit's premier location, in July 2011, Whole Foods Market, a national natural and organic foods supermarket chain, announced it will open a store in Midtown, one block away from Woodward Avenue, in 2013.[22] The population gains and the income level in the area caught the chain's eye. Although smaller than its regular supermarkets, the Midtown store will be a full-service outlet. With the cost to build the store and related expenses estimated at $10.7 million, the site's developer, not Whole Foods, will receive a variety of financial incentives, including $1.2 million in federal tax credits, $1.5 million in state incentives, $500,000 in inducements from Wayne County, as well as $1.5 million in private-foundation funding, with Whole Foods receiving a discount on the rent. The store will strengthen Midtown as a viable residential neighborhood, help attract other retailers, bring some sixty to seventy-five new jobs, and offer better retail food choices to residents.

However, it is unclear whether the growing prosperity in areas such as Midtown can help revitalize other parts of the city. As noted in chapter 1, Detroit reverts increasingly to an urban prairie.

Financial Incentives to Encourage Repopulation

In 2008, the Hudson-Webber Foundation added the 15 × 15 strategy to its agenda. To implement its physical revitalization mission focused on greater downtown Detroit and its efforts to support the housing and retail needs of a young, talented population, the strategy seeks to increase the area's residents by 15,000 households by 2015.[23] So far, two programs, Live Midtown and Live Downtown, exist to draw people, especially those under the age of thirty-five with four-year college degrees or more, to live and work in parts of the city.

A combination of nonprofit institutions, foundations, and a public-sector agency created the Live Midtown residential program in January 2011.[24] Directed at some 30,000 employees of the Detroit Medical Center, the Henry Ford Health System, and Wayne State University, the program offers incentives for individuals and families to purchase or rent in four areas: Midtown, New Center, Virginia Park, and Woodbridge. The inducements include: a $25,000 loan forgivable at once (or $5,000 a year over five years) for buying a primary residence; $5,000 in matching funds for exterior home improvements for existing homeowners working on projects of $10,000 or more; $2,500 for new renters in the first year and an additional $1,000, the second year; and $1,000 for existing renters to renew a lease.

The Live Midtown program earmarked about $1.2 million in 2011 for residential purchasers and renters. The three institutions with employees receiving the incentives each chipped in $200,000 with additional funds from the Hudson-Webber Foundation, The Kresge Foundation, and the Michigan State Housing Development Authority.

The program proved to be a huge hit. By the end of 2011, some 256 employees had taken advantage of the Live Midtown financial incentives.

With the program extended in 2012, the Detroit Medical Center, the Henry Ford Health System, and Wayne State University agreed to each contribute another $200,000 in funding. The Hudson-Webber Foundation and The Kresge Foundation provided additional funds.[25]

Taking a cue from the Live Midtown program, in July 2011, five firms—Quicken Loans, Inc., Compuware Corp., Blue Cross Blue Shield of Michigan, Strategic Staffing Solutions, Inc., and DTE Energy Co.—unveiled the Live Downtown initiative.[26] The Live Downtown plan offers a similar set of incentives for home buyers, exterior property improvements by existing homeowners, and new and existing renters.

The five firms offered these cash incentives to about 16,000 of their full-time and part-time employees to buy (or renovate) homes or rent residences within the boundaries of the downtown central business district; Corktown; Eastern Market; Lafayette Park; Midtown; and Woodbridge neighborhoods. The respective number of eligible employees is as follows: Blue Cross, 6,100; Quicken Loans, 4,000; DTE Energy, 3,000; Compuware, 2,000; and Strategic Staffing Solutions, 500 (including contract workers for the last firm).

The companies pledged some $5 million over five years (2011–16) to encourage their employees to live in the designated areas. In making the five-year commitment, each firm funded the program for $200,000 for the first year. The Hudson-Webber Foundation contributed about $140,000 to cover administrative costs.

Through the employer-provided financial incentives for their respective employees, the Live Downtown program hopes to create a twenty-four-hour living, working, and shopping environment in the six hopefully growing neighborhoods filled with more affluent residents. The developers of the initiative, which seeks to recruit additional companies as sponsors, expect the program to help attract and retain talented workers; spark retail development; reignite the population growth the greater downtown area had experienced before the Great Recession[27]; and lead to the conversion of more office buildings into multi-family residences. Viewing the initiative within the context of the Detroit Works Project, Mayor Bing noted, "This program [Live Downtown] will help create the density that Detroit's downtown needs."[28]

The Live Midtown and Live Downtown residential incentive programs offer the possibility of not only repopulating various neighborhoods but also for stabilizing, if not increasing, home values in these areas. However, tight inventory has hindered the Live Midtown program. Many more individuals and families were interested in the program, but they were dissatisfied with what was available. Apart from the limited funds provided by the sponsor-collaborators, Midtown and other areas need additional newly constructed or renovated residential inventory, drawing on the conversion of empty office buildings. According to Detroit realtors, "To get more people to want to buy, we need more options."[29]

Dan Gilbert's vision may prove to be correct. As noted earlier in this chapter, he wants to make downtown the lively core of a revitalized city, what he calls Detroit 2.0, the center for brain-economy businesses and their knowledge-worker employees. He dreams of forming a downtown residential neighborhood with offices within walking distance of restaurants, stores, and nightlife. According to Gilbert, "That's where young people coming out of universities want to be. I know it's going to work."[30] Again, it is a question of density. The Live Midtown and Live Downtown incentives, as well as other future efforts, need to encourage at least 10,000, if not 20,000 to 30,000, more people to live in the designated areas for a truly sustainable downtown.[31] At present, despite the supply obstacles, the long-awaited upswing for core areas in Detroit seems in progress.

The Need for Public-Private Partnerships

To spark economic growth and help solve tough public problems, such as infrastructure challenges, a need exists for public-private partnerships. These collaborations will involve the public sector, the for-profit private sector, nonprofit organizations, and foundations. Despite its collapse, the M-1 Light Rail project offers a harbinger for future Detroit public-private partnerships.

Today, Detroit faces a number of infrastructure challenges, notably: a lack of mass transit. Cars provide the only reliable means of transportation within the metro Detroit area.

Change on the public transit front seemed to be on the way in 2010 and 2011. Optimism existed—only to be dashed—that the long-discussed plans to build a light rail system, the M-1 Light Rail, along the Woodward Avenue commercial corridor from downtown to the city's northern boundary, 8 Mile Road, might come to fruition. The complex undertaking became mired in the mix of a fiscally constrained city with a bad history of mishandling federal aid and mismanaging public-private partnership projects.

Upward momentum existed from mid-2010, when Detroit took control of the M-1 Light Rail project with the transfer of a title grant from the State of Michigan to the city, until mid-2011. Municipal officials sought a convenient and reliable transit option to stimulate clusters of commercial and residential development along Woodward Avenue. Viewing the project as bringing economic growth along the light rail line, Mayor Bing stated, "We see transportation as a vehicle for development."[32] Besides transporting employees to work downtown, the rail line would help tourists to enjoy the city's sports venues, cultural institutions, its riverfront, and connect many of Detroit's most important institutions along Woodward Avenue.

Optimism increased further in January 2011, when federal officials announced a grant agreement signed by the Federal Transit Administration, the City of Detroit, and the Michigan Department of Transportation for $25 million in federal funds for the M-1 Light Rail line.[33] The $25 million grant came from the $1.5 billion fund for surface transportation, the Transportation Investment Generating Economic Recovery (TIGER) Fund, available under the 2009 federal American Recovery and Reinvestment Act.

As a public-private partnership, the M-1 project would have received additional backing from the public sector: a $300 million grant from the Federal Transit Administration; various other federal and state grants; and funds from the Detroit Downtown Development Authority, a public-sector agency that supports private investment and business growth in the city's central business district. One hundred million dollars would have come from private sources, such as The Kresge Foundation that pledged $35 million to the project, as well as grants from the M-1 Rail Group of corporate leaders, including Roger Penske (motorsports mogul and CEO of The Penske Group), the Ilitch family (pizza and sports and entertainment magnates), Peter Karmanos Jr. (Compuware CEO), and Dan Gilbert. Detroit planned to use the $100 million in private funds as its 20 percent portion of the project's funding and issue $75 million in bonds as seed money for the federal funds.

After numerous discussions with private backers, who had pledged $100 million toward the rail line's construction, in June 2011, the city and the federal government signed off on the details of the $528 million line with nineteen stops along the 9-mile route between downtown and 8 Mile Road. The June 2011 final environmental impact statement spelled out the route and where the stations would be located along the route.[34]

The planned route represented a compromise between business interests—who wanted it to run closer to the curb with frequent stops to facilitate economic development, with riders able to get off the trains at the curb in front of retailers—and transit advocates who favored a line in the center of Woodward Avenue with its dedicated track, providing a speedier system for commuters. The route was planned to run in the center north of Grand Circus Park, but nearer the curb through downtown, giving businesses many stops in the city center.

Optimism proved fleeting, however, as the mayor and the city council battled over control of the Woodward Light Rail Construction Authority, the board that would have overseen the project.[35] The authority's tasks would have included the hiring of technical and engineering staff to supervise the rail line's construction and managing the public and private funds for the project. Mirroring their budget battles, considered in chapter 3, in July 2011, the city council balked at a board composed of the mayor, the city council president, and three mayoral appointees. Thereafter, in September 2011, Mayor Bing turned over control of the project to the Detroit Economic Growth Corp. (DEGC), a quasi-governmental nonprofit organization that spearheads economic development projects for the city. The mayor appoints DEGC board members with the city council's approval. DEGC professionals act as staff for a number of public authorities, including the Detroit Downtown Development Authority. Using common staff, the DEGC coordinates the work of these public authorities and avoids duplication. The DEGC also manages various economic development efforts funded by private and foundation sources.[36]

In the fall of 2011, doubts surfaced about the project's viability, particularly in the context of the city's precarious financial situation. No way existed for Detroit to pay for the estimated $10 million in annual operating costs. Without a dedicated, additional revenue source, such as a tax, the system could not cover its projected operating deficit. Also, the construction budget ballooned from somewhat in excess of $500 million to nearly $600 million, leaving a huge construction budget gap, approaching $100 million. Simply stated, a financially troubled Detroit could not afford to build and operate the proposed 9-mile, M-1 project.

Finally, in December 2011, Mayor Bing and the US Department of Transportation abandoned plans to build the light rail line.[37] Instead, they proposed a less expensive plan for a network of buses to deliver city residents to suburban jobs. The 110-mile bus rapid transit (BRT) system would connect Detroit with its three surrounding counties. The rapid transit buses would be longer than typical buses, with accordion-like middle sections. They would run on their own dedicated lanes, separated from other vehicles, and control traffic signals, thereby avoiding the need to stop at red lights. With fewer stops, the rapid transit buses would hopefully provide more reliable service than the existing regular buses.

The estimated $500 million BRT plan would be funded, in part, by $6.5 million in Federal Transit Administration planning funds together with at least another $300 million in federal funds. Because Detroit's commercial boulevards are so wide, rapid transit buses could easily be added within these existing streets. Outside the city, the network would run on major roads in southeast Michigan, thereby avoiding the building of a substantial amount of new highways. The plan rests, however, on the Michigan legislature approving a regional transit authority, which it did in December 2012, and on voters in southeast Michigan authorizing a tax increase, perhaps a $40 to $60 annual rise in motor vehicle registration fees, to provide additional funds for the system's construction and operation.

The new regional transit authority with representatives from Detroit and its suburbs will operate and manage the proposed system, thereby offering the promise of greater cooperation between the two existing publicly owned bus providers. Under a single regional master transit plan, the new authority will coordinate routes, schedules, and fares between the Detroit Department of Transportation (DDOT) and the Suburban Mobility Authority for Regional Transportation (SMART) bus systems, hopefully eliminating or reducing service overlap and duplication.

The BRT plan would appear to meet the Detroit metro area's regional mass transit needs in a cost-effective manner, connecting downtown with Macomb and Oakland counties as well as the Detroit Metropolitan Wayne County Airport, some twenty-one miles west of downtown, and the Wayne county suburbs. Following the pattern with respect to the Cobo Center,[38] a need exists for the city and its suburbs to end their wasteful bickering and act as one on major issues such as bus transportation that crosses boundaries. Improved access to public transit will help overcome the spatial mismatch between the location of jobs and people.

Undaunted, the privately backed M-1 Rail Group pushed ahead in 2012 for a shorter 3.4-mile light rail line from the riverfront up Woodward Avenue to the New Center area, hoping to promote growth along the corridor connecting the city's most vital business and civic areas and its prime arts, entertainment, and sports venues.[39] Proponents maintained that the private light rail line and the public BRT could coexist and complement each other. They estimated the light rail line would cost some $137 million to build. In addition to private funding from for-profit firms, foundations, nonprofit organizations, and a pledge from the Wayne County government, backers received $25 million in federal grants and hoped to obtain some $15 million in various tax credits. The Kresge Foundation continued to be the project's largest donor at $35 million. The M-1 Rail Group also received pledges of at least $3 million each from Quicken Loans, the Ilitich organization, The Penske Corp., Compuware, the Detroit Medical Center, the Henry Ford Health System, and Wayne State University. Other major supporters include Chevrolet, Chrysler, Blue Cross Blue Shield of Michigan, and the Ford, Kellogg, and Hudson-Webber foundations. After pledging to shoulder 80 percent of the operating costs for the first ten years, the private group then would convey the rail line to the proposed regional transit public authority.

Revitalizing Detroit rests on more than established for-profit businesses and public-private partnerships. Entrepreneurs, and, to a more limited extent, the Creative Class will likely play a key role, particularly with respect to job creation.

Notes

1.   Compuware Corp., "Company History," <www.compuware.com/about/company-history.html> (December 29, 2011).
2.   Quoted in John Gallagher, "Tech hub forms downtown," *Detroit Free Press*, June 10, 2010, B5.

3. Quicken Loans, Inc. (Quicken), Press Release, "Quicken Loans and Sister Companies Move to Downtown Detroit," August 16, 2010 <www,quickenloans.com/about/press-room> (November 23, 2011); Quicken, Press Release, "Quicken Loan Announces Sister Company Quizzle to Relocate to Detroit, " August 4, 2010 <www.quickenloans.com/about/press-room> (November 22, 2011); Quicken, Press Release, "One Reverse Mortgage to Move to Detroit," July 21, 2010 <www.quickenloans.com/about/press-room> (November 23, 2011); Quicken, Press Release, "In-House Realty Announces Plans to Relocate to Detroit, " July 7, 2010 <www.quickenloans.com/about/press-room> (November 23, 2011); Quicken, Press Release, "Fathead, LLC Announces Plans to Move Headquarters to Downtown Detroit This Summer," March 11, 2010 <www.quickenloans.com/about/press-room> (November 23, 2011).

4. Quicken, Press Release, "Quicken Loans Begins Move of 2,500 Additional Team Members to Heart of Downtown Detroit," October 10, 2011 <www.quickenloans.com/about/press-room> (November 23, 2011).

5. Title Source Inc., Press Release, "Rock Holdings' Title Source Moving 1,500 Team Members to Downtown Detroit's First National Building," July 25, 2012. See also John Gallagher, "1,500 jobs moving downtown," *Detroit Free Press*, July 24, 2012, A1, and Karl Henkel, "Quicken Loans' unit sends 1,500 to Detroit," *Detroit News*, July 24, 2012, A1.

6. Quoted in John Gallagher, "Tech hub" and John Gallagher, "Gilbert's Vision," *Detroit Free Press*, June 21, 2011. See also John Gallagher, "Dan Gilbert: the next Mr. Detroit?," *Detroit Free Press*, June 30, 2011, A1. For background on Gilbert see Quicken, Press Release, "Dan Gilbert," n.d. <www.quickenloans.com/press-room/leadership-team/dan-gilbert> (June 27, 2012), and Laura Bennan, "Detroit Needs Business, Can This Man Bring It Back?" *Fortune* 160:10 (November 23, 2009); 73–76.

7. Amy Lane, "Quicken Loans' move tops list of state tax incentives approved by MEGA board," *Crain's Detroit Business*, July 21, 2009 <www.crainsdetroit.com/article/20090721/ FREE/907219993/quicken-loans-move-tops-list> (June 28, 2012).

8. Quicken, Press Release, "Rock Ventures to Finalize Purchase of Detroit's Historic Federal Reserve Building," January 30, 2012 <www.quicken.loans.com/press-room> (June 27, 2012); Quicken, Press Release, "Rock Ventures Group Caps Year of Real Estate Investments in Downtown Detroit with Three Purchases," December 27, 2011 <www.quickenloans.com/press-room> (June 27, 2012); Quicken, Press Release, "Quicken Loans' Group Buys Chase Tower and Two Detroit Center Garage," April 7, 2011 <www.quickenloans.com/about/press-room> (November 23, 2011); Quicken, Press Release, "Quicken Loans' Group Buys Madison Theatre Building," January 26, 2011 <www.quickenloans.com/about/press-room> (November 23, 2011). See also Louis Aguilar, "Gilbert buys ninth downtown building," *Detroit News*, January 31, 2012, A1; John Gallagher, "Giving Detroit a digital hub," *Detroit Free Press*, January 31, 2012, C1; Louis Aguilar, "Gilbert buys another building in Detroit," *Detroit News*, December 14, 2011, C1; Daniel Duggan, "The real deal," *Crain's Detroit Business* 27:34 (August 22, 2011): 1; John Gallagher, "Another Gilbert deal?," *Detroit Free Press*, July 15, 2011, A10;

Maura Webber Sandovi, "Downtown Detroit Dream," *Wall Street Journal,* July 13, 2011, C6; Louis Aguilar, "Quicken adds to Detroit holdings," *Detroit News,* June 1, 2011, C1; Tim Devaney, "Quicken Loans' buys a downtown building," *Detroit News,* January 27, 2011, B4.

9. Tim Devaney, "IT firm expands new Detroit branch," *Detroit News,* September 30, 2010, B6; *Detroit Free Press,* "GalexE. Solutions to add space," September 30, 2010, B5; Gallagher, "Tech hub;" Laura Berman, "Third World aura draws businesses to Detroit," *Detroit News,* July 22, 2010, A4.

10. Blue Cross Blue Shield of Michigan (BCBSM), Press Release, "Blue Cross Blue Shield of Michigan move to downtown Detroit's Renaissance Center hits halfway mark," July 13, 2011 <news.bcbsm.com/news/2011/news_2011-07-13-11023.shtml> (November 30, 2011); BCBSM, Press Release, "Blue Cross Blue Shield of Michigan begins relocation of nearly 3,000 suburban workers to downtown Detroit," May 2, 2011 <news.bcbsm.com/news/2011/news_2011-05-02-12014.shtml> (November 30, 2011); BCBSM, Press Release, "Blue Cross Blue Shield of Michigan announces dates for move of 3,000 employees to Downtown Detroit," January 6, 2011 <news.bcbsm.com/news/2011/news_2011-01-06-15292.shtml> (November 30, 2011). See also Louis Aguilar, "Blues move boosts Detroit," *Detroit News,* July 30, 2010, A16; John Gallagher, "Blue Cross on target in Detroit move," *Detroit Free Press,* July 14, 2011, B5; Louis Aguilar, "3,000 Blues workers start to move to RenCen," *Detroit News,* May 3, 2011, A1.

11. For background on the Renaissance Center, a civic gesture by Henry Ford II, conceived after the 1967 riots, see Bernard J. Frieden and Lynne B. Sagalyn, *Downtown, Inc., How America Rebuilds Cities* (Cambridge, MA: MIT, 1989), 221–222, 332.

12. John Gallagher, "DTE latest to shift staff downtown," *Detroit Free Press,* July 16, 2011, C1, and Melissa Burden, "DTE to relocate 300 employees downtown," *Detroit News,* July 28, 2011, B7.

13. Greg Gardner, "Ad venture to bring 280 jobs to city," *Detroit Free Press,* March 28, 2012, C1, and Melissa Burden, "Chevy to move ads to new company," *Detroit News,* March 28, 2012, C2.

14. Louis Aguilar and Bryce G. Hoffman, "Chrysler makes firm commitment to Detroit," *Detroit News,* May 1, 2012, A7; John Gallagher, "Chrysler move celebrated," *Detroit Free Press,* May 1, 2012, C1; Bruce G. Hoffman and Louis Aguilar, "Chrysler makes downtown move," *Detroit News,* April 26, 2012, A1.

15. Aguilar and Hoffman, "Chrysler makes firm commitment."

16. Louis Aguilar, "Woodward comeback on road to reality," *Detroit News,* June 21, 2012, B1.

17. Jennifer Conlin, "Detroit Pushes Back with Young Muscles," *New York Times,* July 1, 2011, Style 6, and Steve Neavling, "Detroit can map out its future with census data," *Detroit Free Press,* April 3, 2011, A6.

18. Louis Aguilar, "Midtown on the move," *Detroit News,* January 25, 2010, A1.

19. Global Detroit, Final Report, August 11, 2010, 16–18.

20. Ibid., 7–8, 12–13, 31.

21. Aguilar, "Midtown," and R. J. King, "Meet Me in Midtown," *DBusiness,* September–October 2009 <www.dbusiness.com> (June 28, 2012).

22. Detroit Economic Growth Corp., Press Release, "Whole Foods Market to Open Store in Midtown Detroit with Help from DEGC's Green Grocer Project," July 28, 2011 <www.degc.org/news.aspx/whole-foods-market-to-open-store-in midtownDetroit> (November 22, 2011). See also John Bussey, "Whole Foods' Detroit Gamble," *Wall Street Journal*, March 9, 2012, B1; John Gallagher, "Store incentives debated," *Detroit Free Press*, July 29, 2011, A12; Louis Aguilar, "Whole Food says yes to a store in city," *Detroit News*, July 28, 2011, B4.

23. Hudson-Webber Foundation, "15 × 15 Initiative" <www.hudson-webber. org/missionvision/15x15-initiative> (June 28, 2012). For background on the foundation see Hudson-Webber Foundation, "About Us-History" <www. hudson-webber.org/about-us/history> (November 22, 2011).

24. University Cultural Center Association, Press Release, "Live Midtown-Residential Incentive Program," January 20, 2011 <www.detroitmidtown. com/05/news> (April 9, 2012); Live Midtown, Program Guidelines, January 25, 2012; Live Midtown, Press Release, "Live Midtown Program a Success!" n.d. <livemidtown.org> (December 28, 2011). See also John Gallagher, "30,000 workers offered money to move to Midtown," *Detroit Free Press*, January 14, 2011, A1, and Melissa Burden, "Workers enticed to settle in Midtown," *Detroit News*, January 14, 2011, A1.

25. Henry Ford Health System, Press Release, "For 2nd Year, Henry Ford Health System Joins Live Midtown Program," January 25, 2012 <www.henryford. com> (April 9, 2012). See also Melissa Burden, "Live Midtown will get more funding," *Detroit News*, January 26, 2012, B4.

26. Live Downtown, Press Release, "Five Detroit Companies Offer Employees Cash Incentives to Live Downtown," July 25, 2011. See also Melissa Burden and Louis Aguilar, "5 firms lure workers to move downtown," *Detroit News*, July 26, 2011, A7; Melissa Burden, "5 firms will offer cash to live downtown," *Detroit News*, July 23, 2011, A2; Louis Aguilar and Melissa Burden, "Quicken explores Detroit incentives," *Detroit News*, June 23, 2011, A1.

27. In a 2006 market analysis, prior to the Great Recession, downtown Detroit was attracting a small group of young, educated, well-off residents. The downtown core gained a tiny increase of 118 residents from 6,141 in 2000 to 6,259 in 2005. The newcomers lived in households with a median income of $50,000, compared to the household income for all downtown residents of $19,800. See Louis Aguilar, "Quicken move inspires hope," *Detroit News*, July 15, 2010, B4.

28. Quoted in Burden and Aguilar, "5 firms."

29. Austin Black quoted in John Gallagher, "Downtown living boosted," *Detroit Free Press*, June 23, 2011, B1. See also Susan Stellin, "New Thirst for Urban Living, and Too Few Detroit Rentals," *New York Times*, December 12, 2012, B8.

30. Quoted in Sadovi, "Downtown Detroit Dream."

31. Mark Talley quoted in Aguilar, "Quicken move inspires."

32. Quoted in Suzette Hackney, "Bing: Nothing final in plan for city," *Detroit Free Press*, May 12, 2010, A2.

33. Federal Transit Administration, Press Release, "U.S. Transportation Secretary LaHood Announces $25 Million Recovery Act Grant Agreement for Detroit Light Rail Project," January 20, 2011 <www.fta.dot.gov> (December 28, 2011).

34. Tom Greenwood and Leonard N. Fleming, "Route OK'd for light rail project," *Detroit News*, June 30, 2011, A1, and Matt Helms, "Woodward light-rail project surges ahead after city, feds agree on a route," *Detroit Free Press*, June 29, 2011, A1.

35. Matt Helms, "Light-rail plans sputter over who will supervise," *Detroit Free Press*, July 14, 2011, A13.

36. Detroit Economic Growth Authority, "How DEGC Works" <www.degc.org/how-degc-works.aspx> (December 29, 2011) and "Partners" <www.degc.org/partners.aspx> (December 29, 2011).

37. Matthew Dolan, "No Train for the Motor City," *Wall Street Journal*, December 16, 2011, A3; Matt Helms, "Rapid transit system what area needs," *Detroit Free Press*, February 25, 2012, A3; Matt Helms, "Bus rapid transit system wins some metro fans," *Detroit Free Press*, February 24, 2012, A6; Matt Helms, "How this transit system differs," *Detroit Free Press*, February 24, 2012, A6; Dave Bing, "Rapid buses are a win for Detroit region," *Detroit Free Press*, December 18, 2011, A23; Matt Helms, Paul Egan, John Gallagher, "Light-rail plan scrapped," *Detroit Free Press*, December 14, 2011, A1; David Shepardson, "Rapid buses bump light rail plan," *Detroit News*, December 14, 2011, A1; David Shepardson and James Lynch, "Light rail supporters to battle on," *Detroit News*, December 15, 2011, A1.

38. One hopeful sign of city-suburb cooperation, a new five-member regional authority, The Detroit Regional Convention Facility Authority, took over control of the Cobo Center in September 2009, as the result of state intervention. The Michigan legislature created the authority and authorized $299 million in funding from hotel, cigarette, and liquor taxes to pay for operations, upgrades, and expansion. A new board enhanced and expanded the center, the host venue for the annual North American International Auto Show, hired a new manager, eliminated widespread corruption that inflated exhibitors' costs, and borrowed some $80 million to fund the makeover. As part of the arrangement, Detroit received $20 million in cash to replace parking revenues that go to the authority, which assumed Detroit's existing debts for the center. Matthew Dolan, "Detroit Arena's Revival Points Way for City," *Wall Street Journal*, April 23, 2012, A7; John Gallagher, "Operating revenues double," *Detroit Free Press*, February 11, 2012, C1; "Cobo financing secured," *Detroit Free Press*, November 10, 2011, B5; Oralandar Brand-Williams, "Major makeover of Cobo Center unveiled," *Detroit News*, March 3, 2011, A1; John Gallagher, "Region makes effort to mend longtime rifts," *Detroit Free Press*, January 21, 2011, A1.

39. Todd Spangler and Matt Helms, "U.S. won't fund Detroit rail—yet," *Detroit Free Press*, June 20, 2012, A1; Matt Helms, "Feds not sold on Woodward light-rail line," *Detroit Free Press*, June 5, 2012, A1; Leonard N. Fleming and David Shepardson, "Backers: M-1 rail funds on track," *Detroit News*, June 5, 2012, A3; David Shepardson, "Light rail cost jumps to $137M," *Detroit News*, April 24, 2012, A1; Matt Helms, "Light-rail group: We have most of money," *Detroit Free Press*, April 24, 2012, A1; David Shepardson, "Feds wary of Detroit's downtown rail plan," *Detroit News*, March 17, 2012, A1; Matt Helms, "Detroit rail line draws doubts," *Detroit Free Press*, March 17, 2012, A1; Matt Helms, "Second chance for light rail," *Detroit Free Press*, January 7, 2012, A1; David Shepardson, "Private support reignites

Woodward light rail plan," *Detroit News*, January 7, 2012, A1; Matt Helms, "Light-rail investors press on with plans to build," *Detroit Free Press*, December 17, 2011, A4; Matt Helms, John Gallagher, Todd Spangler, "Investors hold out hope for light rail," *Detroit Free Press*, December 15, 2011, A1; David Shepardson and James Lynch, "Light rail supporters to battle on," *Detroit News*, December 15, 2011, A1.

7

Economic Development through Entrepreneurship and the Creative Class

Entrepreneurs will likely play a major role in Detroit's revitalization, together with the Creative Class, a subset of entrepreneurs. These small enterprises, if successful, offer a reliable way of making a living. It is hard work for the first few years, with a high failure rate, but it offers a path for some to economic self-sufficiency, enabling those who can create and manage a small business to support themselves and their families, as well as create jobs for others. A few may blossom into large firms, employing thousands.

To foster entrepreneurship, Detroit's public sector must encourage start-up and small-business growth, thereby overcoming its reputation as a difficult city in which to start and do business. If it can surmount this obstacle, which seems likely, the city will attract new investments, create jobs, and expand its tax base.[1] Also, the support system, in terms of capital, space, and training, is becoming more robust for entrepreneurs.

This chapter also considers the possible role of the Creative Class in facilitating economic growth. Although widely touted as an economic development and job creation engine, the Creative Class seems destined to play a far more limited role than entrepreneurship, more generally. Moreover, the Creative Class will likely perpetuate the city's racial divide.

This chapter also analyzes Detroit's human capital challenge, one of the biggest obstacles to the city's revitalization. Simply put, a mismatch exists between available jobs, now and likely in the future, and adult residents' skills and education levels. It urges the public sector, foundations, and wealthy individuals to allocate more funds to organizations seeking to improve residents' basic skills—thereby enabling them to gain jobs in low-skill-oriented retail and service businesses, and provide training in growing areas, such as technology and health care. However, the bleak track record of past and current training efforts, generally, only offers a low possibility of success.

Entrepreneurship as a Path to Economic Growth

Entrepreneurship has become a focus for Detroit's revitalization in coming decades. These start-ups represent a key to Detroit's economic development. To achieve future economic growth, entrepreneurship must bubble up from the ground, in people's homes and tiny offices.

Entrepreneurs seek to make a profit, grow their businesses, and increase their income and wealth. To make themselves more affluent, they must make or do something that others want. As the desire grows for their goods or services, their businesses, in turn, expand to meet the demand. Firms hire more people, providing livelihoods for a few, and perhaps for hundreds and thousands. In addition to fueling job creation and making neighborhoods more attractive to potential residents, new businesses boost the city's revenue stream.

Detroit has long served as a hub of black entrepreneurship.[2] In the 1960s and 1970s, as blacks populated the city, they took the skills they gained from working for white-owned firms to start and build their own businesses: hotels, auto dealerships, construction companies, and architectural firms. As was true of many cities, the entrepreneurial spirit ran families, even if the next generation earned college (and even advanced) degrees.

For a long time, however, Detroit's for-profit private sector relied on a large-firm economy, marked by megafactories serving the auto industry. As a result, the local entrepreneurial culture, particularly among blacks, remained underdeveloped, with the city among the least entrepreneurial places in the nation.[3]

Today, building a broad-based entrepreneurial culture represents a difficult challenge. A cultural shift must occur from, for example, the traditional big-firm corporate culture oriented around employment with an auto-related company to an entrepreneurial culture, one embracing risk and innovation in return for possible rewards. Building this new culture involves taking a chance on launching a new endeavor and, if it fails, moving forward to something new. It involves lifelong learning, the constant study of unmet consumer desires, and the acquisition of new skills.

In this century's second decade, business start-ups in Detroit are popping up in pockets due to affordable rent, ample space, and a growing community of entrepreneurs and creative types, both of whom see the opportunity to take risks they could not assume in many other metropolitan areas.[4] For example, the Riverwalk, the green space along the Detroit River, attracts people interested in recreational activities, drawing more new businesses to the area. The Motor City is turning into a cycling city. Two young women created Wheelhouse Detroit, a bike store.

Providing Capital, Space, and Training for Entrepreneurs

Besides discovering the entrepreneurial spirit and finding a niche, an unmet or undermet need, would-be entrepreneurs require capital, space, and training for their business start-ups.

Meeting Capital Needs

Often, fledgling enterprises require relatively modest sums to get started. In addition to tapping family, friends, and their credit cards, crowdfunding, a nascent venture capital industry, foundations, and microloan programs now offer other possible capital sources.

Crowdfunding. Crowdfunding enables investors to support small businesses through the Internet, thereby democratizing investment and access to capital. Using a web-based crowdfunding portal or a broker, an entrepreneur can start a campaign to secure funding for his or her concept. Brokers or online funding portals, registered with the US Securities and Exchange Commission, take a commission on the funds raised. If individuals are willing to invest in an unproved idea, the owner-entrepreneur, with a strong local following, can show it is a promising concept and possibly obtain further funding. Crowdfunding also enables entrepreneurs to create a buzz about a product or service.

Crowdfunding received an important boost in 2012 with the enactment of the federal JOBS (Jumpstart Our Business Startups) Act.[5] In brief, small firms can sell equity stakes online to a large number of investors. Under the new rules, a business can raise up to $1 million during any twelve-month period. Individuals with incomes or net worth below $100,000 can invest 5 percent of their income, up to a $2,000 maximum, per company per year. Businesses will no longer face the usual US Securities and Exchange Commission rules that come with larger offerings, such as the level of disclosure found in a traditional prospectus. However, firms must provide investors, through brokers or funding portals; certain information, including a description of the business; the intended use of proceeds; the firm's ownership and capital structure; and financial statements. If a company wants to raise less than $100,000, its CEO must certify the truthfulness of its financial statements and provide investors with the firm's prior-year federal income tax return. To raise between $100,000 and $500,000, a business must provide financial statements reviewed by an independent certified public accountant. An offering in excess of $500,000 requires audited financial statements.

Venture Capital Firms. For start-ups, particularly tech companies, venture capital firms can provide another source of funds to promising companies ready to expand rapidly. After relying on a few giant corporations, a more entrepreneurial business model is slowly coming to Michigan.

The number of venture capital deals done in a state serves as one indicator of entrepreneurial activity. Venture capital transactions in Michigan peaked in 2000 with fifty-five deals totaling $286 million in equity investments. The number fell during the Great Recession with the state seeing thirty-three deals worth $152 million in 2010, only to fall to thirty-one deals valued at $83 million in 2011, a fourteen-year low.[6]

To help fill the capital gap and implement Dan Gilbert's vision of making Detroit a high-tech hub, Detroit Venture Partners (DVP) now offers financing (so-called seed money) to promising start-up and early-stage technology firms—with a bias toward Detroit-area companies.[7] Gilbert—along with Josh Linker, the founder (and former chairman) of ePrize, a suburban Detroit-based online firm that creates promotional campaigns, online sweepstakes, and points-based loyalty programs, and Brian Hamlin, the founder and chairman of Rockbridge Growth Equity, a private equity firm—launched DVP in November 2010. Linker serves as DVP's managing partner. In July 2011, basketball legend Earvin (Magic) Johnson joined DVP.[8]

DVP's goal focuses on creating Gilbert's hoped-for technology corridor downtown where professionals can live, work, and play. The firm expects to complete fifteen deals annually by financing technology companies, especially e-commerce and social media firms, that can help rebuild the city and the region. It looks to invest initially $250,000 to $750,000, with a total investment of $2 million to $3 million, if a company evidences strong performance. Bankrolling a total of some $100 million in a few years could create thousands of new technology jobs.

Foundations. Looking to rebuilding Detroit through entrepreneurship, foundations can play a role. They can buy stock or make loans to a commercial venture, provided the firm's activities promote the foundation's charitable objectives as program-related investments (PRIs).[9] Talented scientists, among others, who work for profit companies, have a financial incentive to make breakthroughs in areas that foundations could consider vital to their charitable missions.

To qualify as a PRI an investment must meet two main criteria. First, the investment's primary purpose must carry out the foundation's charitable objective. Second, no significant purpose of the investment can be to generate income or capital appreciation. Stated differently, the investment must be on terms that would be unattractive to an investor purely motivated by profit. PRIs generally count in meeting a foundation's requirement to distribute 5 percent of its capital each year.

Microlending. Foundations and wealthy individuals can also help by creating microloan programs. Modeled after the strategy pioneered by the Grameen Bank, these no-collateral loan funds, particularly those requiring participants to save money and invest wisely to grow their businesses, provide another source of start-up and operational capital.[10]

In Detroit, for example, the Detroit Micro-Enterprise Fund and the First Step Fund provide microloans to start-ups and entrepreneurs.[11] Kiva.org, an online lending platform for small Third World businesses, launched its first US lending arm, Kiva Detroit. The Michigan Corps, a group of local and expatriate Michiganders seeking to help the state, brought together Kiva.org, Accion USA (an established national microlender) and a $250,000 matching pledge from the John S. and James L. Knight Foundation, to fund Kiva Detroit.[12]

Providing Space and Training

A need also exists for providing would-be entrepreneurs with office and lab space, as well as training to help them grow. In Detroit, two helpful resources, among others, for aspiring business founders exist: TechTown, one of the world's largest business incubators, and Gilbert's entrepreneurial boot camp, Bizdom U.

TechTown represents one of Wayne State University's (WSU) most ambitious and significant efforts to go beyond educating students and help rebuild Detroit.[13] Active in the city's revitalization, WSU envisioned TechTown, more formally, the Wayne State University Research and Technology Park, as a research and technology park that fosters the growth of small businesses in the city. Although an independent nonprofit organization, WSU officials were (and continue to be) closely involved in TechTown's creation (in partnership with General Motors and the Henry Ford Health System), growth, and current activities. WSU provided some $2.7 million to TechTown between 2007 and 2011, or about 23 percent of its programmatic funding.[14]

TechTown opened in April 2004,[15] funded by $12 million provided, in part, from The Kresge Foundation and the New Economy Initiative for Southeast Michigan. Previously, in 2003, General Motors donated TechTown's 100,000-square-foot, five-story building to the venture. Originally constructed in 1927, the building is perched south of Detroit's New Center neighborhood, at the edge of WSU's campus.

TechTown functions as a business incubator, helping foster innovation and entrepreneurship.[16] It has become Detroit's most sought-after address for start-ups, ranging from low- and high-tech firms, well-funded research laboratories, and nonprofit arts organizations. Today, about 80 percent of TechTown's 250 companies are lifestyle microenterprises, focusing on the delivery of goods and services in Detroit. It not only provides office space and supplies, but also offers one of the nation's most aggressive business-incubator programs, providing training to owners through entrepreneurial seminars, mentoring, and support staff and connecting them with additional resources outside the organization. Since 2008, more than 2,200 people have received various types of entrepreneurial training, such as its FastTrac program, through TechTown. It has also introduced some 8,000 Michigan residents to the new entrepreneurial culture through public events and walk-in sessions. Some of these attendees went on to set up their own firms outside the TechTown building.

It also helps companies raise capital, with more than 100 businesses having successfully obtained funds with TechTown's support. Through the TechTown Loan Fund and its Thrive One Fund, TechTown has invested some $700,000 in early-stage companies. It has helped clients amass $14 million in follow-on funding from various investment funds.

With its main building completely filled, TechTwo, the long-awaited expansion of TechTown, opened in February 2011.[17] TechTwo provides additional space for cultivating businesses to remake the auto-era industrial stronghold into a hub for information technology and biotechnology. It also hopes to lure entrepreneurs working in advertising, real estate, and public relations, among other fields.

In meeting the need for office space, TechTwo offers low-cost leases for offices, cubicles, and even mailboxes. It hopes to draw more young, tech-oriented entrepreneurs than TechTown. To attract these individuals, TechTwo also provides hoteling space, where people can sit anywhere and work. It features a small art gallery surrounded by an outdoor meeting spot.

WSU purchased the 110,000-square-foot TechTwo building for $1 million in December 2009. The eighty-four-year-old, three-story structure underwent retrofitting to transform the former Cadillac dealership into an office space start-up hub for 200 to 300 entrepreneurs. The cost of the renovation amounted to $10 million, with commitments for nearly $6 million received from the public sector, including Wayne County and several federal government agencies, and from foundations. The Kresge Foundation made an $800,000 grant to support the creation of TechTwo.[18] Also, in October 2010, a commercial bank, the Bank of Ann Arbor, lent TechTown funds, guaranteed by WSU, to expand the business incubator's operations. Proceeds of the ten-year loan will fund TechTwo's operations.[19]

Besides helping start-ups and other businesses, TechTown and Tech-Two offer other benefits. For the surrounding neighborhood, TechTwo, for example, has been a boon. It will better connect the New Center area with nearby Midtown, a neighborhood to the south, and make it a more walkable corridor lined with shops and other businesses.

In addition to TechTown and TechTwo, in April 2010, WSU and the business-focused Walsh College established the Blackstone LaunchPad to spur undergraduate students to start their own businesses in the Detroit area.[20] The effort was funded by a $2 million grant from the Blackstone Charitable Foundation, as part of the $50 million Blackstone Entrepreneurship Initiative. Founded at the University of Miami in 2008, the LaunchPad program, housed in career placement centers, allows students to test their start-up ideas on their peers, faculty, and local business coaches.

Besides capital and space, would-be business founders need training. Dan Gilbert founded Bizdom U, a nonprofit organization offering entrepreneurial training, in 2007.[21] As an elite organization for aspiring entrepreneurs, it trains, mentors, and funds individuals to open growth-oriented, innovative Detroit-based businesses.

Bizdom U now offers two distinct programs: Idea Generator and Launch Labs. In the Idea Generator program, students with an idea for a new business receive accelerated training to break down an idea and turn it into a business, or go back to the drawing board. For those who have a business idea they want to explore, but are not ready to devote their lives to pursuing it, training is offered two to three nights a week and on one or two Saturdays over an eight-week period. If a student's business model proves viable, he or she has the opportunity to seek funding if accepted into Bizdom U's Launch Labs.

Those who have completed the Idea Generator program—as well as other entrepreneurs with a well-developed, customer-focused, scalable operational model, who are ready to build a prototype or a full-fledged business—can seek entry into Bizdom U's Launch Labs program. If accepted into this program, Bizdom will invest $10,000 plus $4,500 per founder in the business in exchange for an 8 percent equity interest. For three months, the program enables a participant to launch his or her business in a collaborative incubator, receive training in various business functions, such as marketing, and coaching and feedback from experienced business and technology experts. At the end of an entrepreneur's participation in the Launch Labs program, Bizdom U places him or her in a room with multiple investors to seek the funding needed to take the business to the next level.

Building Human Capital

Entrepreneurially led economic growth will help fuel job creation and may reduce Detroit's chronically high unemployment levels. However, innovative firms, in fields such as information technology and biotechnology, may offer few job opportunities for Detroit residents lacking basic reading, writing, math, and digital skills. Large portions of the Detroit workforce are not prepared for new knowledge-based, information-technology positions that will replace the manufacturing jobs that have disappeared. Thus, a need exists to build the human capital of Detroit residents, many of whom have limited education, job skills, and workforce attachment.

Local adult-learning resources to improve basic skills, especially those that relate to careers in emerging Detroit-based tech firms, are extremely limited. One study showed that less than 10 percent of those lacking basic skills received the help they needed.[22] Furthermore, even the 10 percent served did not receive services over any significant time frame or achieve any positive learning outcomes. The majority of the programs offered related neither to individuals' occupational interests nor future employment prospects, thereby continuing to isolate Detroiters from economic opportunities. Most programs lacked any meaningful connections to employers, such as on-site learning opportunities, contacts with potential employment openings, or feedback on a skill-building curriculum. The vast majority of programs also failed to: offer intensive instructional formats that enabled adults to improve their skills; allow learners to earn, while engaged in learning, through transitional job programs or paid internships; or provide supportive services, such as transportation or child care, for learners.

To tackle the human capital challenge, in 2010, a coalition of public-sector agencies and nonprofits, including foundations and community-based organizations, launched ten learning labs in Detroit to teach adults the basic skills they need to obtain and retain jobs.[23] Serving only some 2,500 learners each year, these labs, however, only meet a fraction of the needed workforce training geared to serve current and future job opportunities.

To better match jobs and skills, the public sector, foundations, and wealthy individuals ought to provide workforce development programs, such as the Detroit Regional Workforce Fund, with additional funds. Given the number of competing priorities, it is uncertain whether additional funds for workforce development will be available. The bleak track record of past and current job-training efforts, generally, offers little hope of success.[24]

One expert has sounded the following cautionary note with respect to job-training programs, generally:

> Since there is little evidence of jobs being newly created for graduates of job training programs, it seems likely that programs indeed serve a purely distributional function. To the extent that this is true, all of the earnings gains provided by all jobs training programs are illusory.[25]

Thus, in the short and intermediate term, it is questionable how much remediation is possible.

On a more positive note, workforce development organizations must look beyond the traditional social-service approach, seeing job seekers as their only customers. They also ought to view businesses as their customers, so as to facilitate employer buy-ins; respond to employer needs; and better analyze future industry trends, identifying sectors that will grow over the long term. These organizations must strive to overcome the existing bureaucratic funding silos.

Funders must emphasize the need for organizational accountability in achieving measurable results. They ought to fund only the best, most effective programs and encourage others to build on these programmatic successes. This is not easy.

Another obstacle to successful workforce development exists. As noted in chapter 1, a mismatch exists, because of job sprawl, between where workers live and where jobs are located.

Even with a vast improvement in basic skills and special training in marketable competencies, for-profit businesses will be unable to absorb all the unemployed, underemployed, and those who have ceased looking for a job. If these individuals do not look for work outside the region, some may turn to entrepreneurship to create their own opportunities. Tapping the entrepreneurial spirit of the unemployed and underemployed, small start-up, for-profit enterprises could produce and sell goods and services for the local market.

The Role of the Creative Class

The Creative Class[26] may play a role in reinventing Detroit. According to one of its leading proponents, members of the Creative Class "engage in work whose function is to 'create meaningful new forms.'"[27] The class consists not only of visual and performing artists, writers, architects, and those in design and fashion, but also knowledge-workers who create new ideas, technology, and/or content. They "share a common creative ethos that values creativity, individuality, difference, and merit."[28]

A thriving arts—more generally creative—community including businesses, nonprofit organizations, and individuals involved in the active, exploratory process—from conception, production, and presentation—could lure others to Detroit with fresh ideas, energy, and new capital. Creativity in all its forms feeds off and leads to more creativity. Apart from its economic impact, an environment pulsating with energy and providing opportunities for talent brings a certain vitality to any city.

The Creative Class in Detroit

The influx of artists has created a fertile and growing creative community in Detroit.[29] Over the past decade, the city has experienced a small, but significant, inbound movement of artists and other innovative types, who found a welcoming, close community of other "creatives" and their supporters. According to the best estimates, at least some 4,000 artists live or work in Detroit.[30]

These artists serve as urban pioneers in neglected, gritty neighborhoods. Drawn by access to affordable studios and living space, they saw empty lots, abandoned houses, and disused factories as unparalleled opportunities. Seeking to push the artistic envelope, visual artists created works in small studios and big warehouses. They turned crumbling homes into residences and art centers. At the Power House Project, artist Mitch Cope and his architect wife Gina Reichert purchased a former drug house for $1,900. Outfitting the one-bedroom bungalow—whose wiring, heating, and plumbing had been stripped—with solar panels and wind turbines, they turned it into a self-reliant, off-the-grid structure that now serves as a residence for visiting artists.[31] Cope and Reichert, along with others, went on to create eight similar structures within a four-block radius, many painted by street artists.

Factories have been converted into studios and exhibition spaces. Dennis Kefallinos, a pizza parlor and strip-club owner, bought the vacant 2.2 million-square-foot Russell Industrial Center, a seven-building complex, for $1.5 million in 2003. Without any help from the public or philanthropic sectors, he converted about 1 million square feet into a cultural complex and studio space for more than one hundred small business tenants, many of whom operate on the frontlines of Detroit's growing creative economy.[32]

With the new energy came the trappings of a thriving, young, adult culture. Trendy bars and restaurants brought pedestrians back to some once-desolate streets.

Innovative funding concepts flourish. A monthly dinner, called Detroit Soup, funds creative proposals through microgrants.[33] Anyone with an innovative project that would benefit the city can present an idea to the group and try to receive money to get the concept off the ground. Guests pay $5 for a bowl of soup, bread, salad, and dessert and listen to four or five pitches for ideas. At the end of the meal, everyone votes and the winner takes home a kitty, normally $600 to $900, to fund his or her project. Detroit Soup spawned other events for awarding grants, such as Friends of Spaulding Court. This group holds monthly gatherings to raise awareness about its project to restore two rows of townhomes in north Corktown, as well as others in the city.[34]

Creativity—more narrowly focused on painting, sculpture, literature, theater, song, dance, film, and the related fields of architecture, design, and fashion—provides a host of economic advantages for urban revitalization. Although exact numbers are unavailable, the benefits of this community for Detroit include some spin-off employment gains, assistance for other small businesses, particularly retailers, enhancement of property values, and a boost for the city's tax base and its image.[35]

The Kresge Foundation and Detroit's Creative Culture

Foundations, led by The Kresge Foundation, see that art matters. Kresge recognized the importance of stimulating the flowering of a creative culture in Detroit. It has funded several notable cultural endeavors, including the Kresge Artist Fellows Program and the biennial Art X Detroit festival.

Beginning in 2009, Kresge has annually funded the Kresge Artist Fellows Program with $25,000 fellowships to: eighteen visual artists, in 2009; eighteen literary and performing artists, in 2010; twelve visual artists, in 2011; and twenty-four literary and performing artists, in 2012.[36] These no-strings-attached grants are among the nation's most lucrative awards for individual artists. The grants seek to nurture metro Detroit's creative class, from relative newcomers to credentialed figures, and keep them from leaving Michigan.

In perhaps its most ambitious effort, designed to catch the eye of local, national, and even international audiences, and show the wealth of creative talent in the Detroit area, Kresge underwrote the April 2011 Art X Detroit.[37] The city had never hosted a quality cultural festival of multidisciplinary sweep and form—encompassing painters, sculptors, composers, musicians, dancers, and poets, with a range of styles, mediums, traditions, expressions, and aesthetic priorities—crossing the generations.

The first Art X Detroit, planned as a biennial festival, trumpeted homegrown culture. Spotlighting Kresge's fellows, the festival gathered thirty-six Kresge artist fellows and two eminent artists in a five-day showcase of the depth and diversity of visual, performing, and literary talent in the Detroit area. More than forty free events were held in a dozen Midtown venues. With the total attendance of 10,000 people, many festival events drew overflow crowds. Art X Detroit boosted the city's image, spotlighted the Midtown neighborhood, helped small businesses, created temporary jobs, and increased the city's sales tax revenues.

The Detroit Creative Corridor Center

One collaborative effort, the Detroit Creative Corridor Center (DC3), seeks to build creative industries in Detroit.[38] Recently, the center launched its Creative Ventures Acceleration Program.

The DC3, a business incubator founded in 2010, focuses its efforts on creative industries, including design, the visual and performing arts, and film. It supplies infrastructure, strategic counseling, and consulting for those wanting to start and grow Detroit-based creative businesses in a variety of fields.

The DC3 represents a partnership between the College for Creative Studies (College), an art school that has served as an active agent in facilitating the city's rebirth, and Business Leaders for Michigan, a group of corporate CEOs, chairpersons, and most senior executives of the state's largest job providers and universities. It is funded, in large part, by the public sector, including the US Small Business Administration and the Michigan Economic Development Corp., and foundations, including the New Economy Initiative for Southeast Michigan, The Kresge Foundation, and the John S. and James L. Knight Foundation. It also generates part of its revenues through fee-based consulting work.

Subsequently, in July 2011, DC3 launched its Creative Ventures Acceleration Program.[39] Designed to assist businesses that have grown past the start-up phase but want to meet a need in Detroit's creative economy, the program selected seventeen early- and second-stage companies to help them flourish in various mass-oriented creative fields, including architecture, film production, and graphic design. The program chose the firms based on their potential to fill a demand in a large market; commitment to grow; and ability to use the resources provided. Thirteen of the firms participated in the ventures-in-residence program offering an in-depth curriculum, physical resources, and work space, together with access to the College's strategic counseling resources. The physical Acceleration Studio and Work Space opened in the summer of 2011 at the College's Taubman Center. Four firms comprise the virtual acceleration program consisting of online tutorials and discussions, as well as monthly open business forums in which participants share best practices. The owners of all seventeen firms are matched with a network of mentors from relevant companies and industry groups.

The Creative Ventures Acceleration Program received $500,000 to fund the initial twelve-month curriculum for the seventeen firms. Funding was provided by the New Economy Initiative for Southeast Michigan, the Michigan Economic Development Corp., and the US Small Business Administration.

The Detroit Creative Corridor Center and its Creative Ventures Acceleration Program represent a major effort to attract and expand businesses in various creative fields. Working with TechTown will facilitate the development of a seamless creative-sector incubation, acceleration, and business-operation model in Detroit. Hopefully, these efforts will also generate jobs for creative-sector workers.

The Potential of the Creative Class

Creative endeavors, like entrepreneurship more generally, do not represent a complete panacea for solving Detroit's ills. They can play a role in revitalizing the city.

At present, it is unclear whether a land of creative, often entrepreneurial, opportunity can spark a citywide renewal or if the creative havens will be confined to limited geographical areas. A need exists for more venues that are neither bars nor major old-line cultural institutions. Foundations, led by Kresge, are trying by funding a multiplicity of endeavors. However, it is unclear how foundations and/or the public sector can leverage the artistic community and the Creative Class, more generally, to spark broad-based economic development and job creation in Detroit.

Race and class enter into the picture. Presenting a significant obstacle, a racial disconnect exists. The largely white Creative Class stands apart from a mostly black populace. So far, integration is rare, thereby continuing the economic marginalization of many Detroit African Americans. Furthermore, critics of the creative economy as a panacea see the Creative Class exacerbating inequality through an unequal social and geographical distribution of benefits.[40] They note, "The expansion of both arts occupations specifically and the creative economy overall will create more opportunities for highly skilled workers than for urban residents with modest educational qualifications."[41]

The Public Sector's Role in Facilitating Entrepreneurship and the Creative Economy

In striving to facilitate entrepreneurship and a creative economy, Detroit must overcome its reputation as a difficult city in which to start and do business. Given the regulatory labyrinth and licensing complexity, it must streamline the process for obtaining approval, licenses, and permits to start and expand small businesses. The city could designate one agency to collect all the submissions required to start a small business in Detroit. The regulatory simplification could take the form of a one-stop public sector website covering all the tax and business license issues, among other administrative matters, and the consolidation of all subsequent reporting requirements. Separately and as a group these represent easy changes to implement, but nothing is simple in Detroit.

To promote entrepreneurship,[42] the city, more generally, needs to reduce, if not eliminate, any antibusiness regulations and attitudes and stimulate more start-ups. Public officials and opinion molders, such as clergy, can no longer view profits, in particular, and businesses, large and small, with suspicion. They must accept the premise that the free market, not the public sector, provides the basis for prosperity and economic growth, traditionally viewed, based on consumption.

With its vacant land and large pool of unskilled labor, Detroit could take an alternative path to revitalization beginning with urban agriculture. Worker-owner, cooperative businesses devoted to meeting basic needs of Detroiters could flourish, despite long odds.

Notes

1. For an assessment of the human-capital challenge facing shrinking cities, such as Detroit, along with policy recommendations and examples of human-capital investments, see Robert Giloth and Jillien Meier, "Human Capital and Legacy Cities," in *Rebuilding America's Legacy Cities: New Directions for the Industrial Heartland,* ed. Alan Mallach (New York: American Assembly, 2012): 190–222.

2. See, e.g., Steven Gray, "Where Entrepreneurs Need Nerves of Steel," *Fortune* 162:6 (October 18, 2010): 63–66. See generally W. Sherman Rogers, *The African American Entrepreneur: Then and Now* (Santa Barbara, CA: Praeger 2010): 81–145.

3. Robert W. Fairlie, Kauffman Index of Entrepreneurial Activity, 1996–2011, Ewing Marion Kauffman Foundation, March 2012, 21 (Table 11 Kauffman Index of Entrepreneurial Activity for the Fifteen Largest MSAs (2011)). See also Katherine Yung, "Entrepreneurial Spirit seen in Detroit" *Detroit Free Press*, March 20, 2012, C1, and John Gallagher, "State lags in start-up," *Detroit Free Press*, March 20, 2012, C2.

4. See, e.g., Louis Aguilar, "Job creators setting up shop," *Detroit* News, April 25, 2012, A1; Jennifer Conlin, "Detroit Pushes Back with Young Muscles," *New York Times*, July 1, 2011, ST6; Milicent Johnson, "Detroit, community resilience and the American dream," *Grist*, January 11, 2011 <www.grist.org/article/2011-01-07> (June 26, 2012).

5. Section 4(6) of the Securities Act of 1933, added by JOBS (Jumpstart Our Business Startups) Act of 2012, Public Law 112-106. See also Angus Loten, "Stalled Crowd funding Rules Leave Business Plans on Ice," *Wall Street Journal*, December 13, 2012, B1; Javier Espinoza, "Doing Equity Crowd Funding Right," *Wall Street Journal*, May 21, 2012, R3; Jonathan Weisman, "Final Approval by House Sends Jobs Bill to President for Signature," *New York Times*, March 28, 2012, A12; Edward Wyatt, "Bill to Aid Start-Ups Is

Approved by Senate," *New York Times*, March 23, 2012, B1; Sarah E. Needleman and Angus Loten, "When 'Friending' Becomes a source of Start-Up Funds," *Wall Street Journal*, November 1, 2011, B1.

Entrepreneurs can also turn to Kickstarter, an online fund-raising site. A business sets a funding goal with funds released only if a project reached its objective. Backers receive a token, such as a T-shirt. Kickstarter takes 5 percent of the final amount achieved and Amazon Payments, which processes the money, takes 3 to 5 percent. Mary Billard, "A Big Push to Get Going," *New York Times*, June 21, 2012, E6, and Andrea Rumbaugh, "Crowdfunding helps companies raise cash," *Detroit* News, July 8, 2011, A8.

Another possibility is peer-to-peer lending, through online vetting platforms such as Lending Club and Prosper, where small business owners with good credit scores can borrow funds from individuals investors, who combine to lend money. The loans are small, however, with a maximum of $35,000 at Lending Club.

6.   Katherine Yung, "State venture capital tumbles to 14-year low," *Detroit Free Press*, January 20, 2012, A12; Katherine Yung, "State's start-ups starve for capital," *Detroit Free Press*, December 1, 2011, B1; John Gallagher, "Start-up results remain modest," *Detroit Free Press*, October 28, 2011, A11.

7.   Detroit Venture Partners, Press Release, "Detroit Venture Partners," n.d. <www.midventures.com/2010/12/15/detroit-venture-partners-aimed-at-startups> (December 7, 2011). See also Jaclyn Trop, "Venture capitalist with a passion for Metro Detroit," *Detroit News*, June 2, 2011, S2.

8.   Melissa Burden and Andrea Rumbaugh, "Magic Johnson joins effort to rebuild Detroit," *Detroit News*, July 22, 2011, A1.

9.   See generally Robert C. Pozen, "Why Not Venture-Capital Philanthropy?," *Wall Street Journal*, June 4, 2012, A15. Proposed regulations provide examples of program-related investments by private foundations. Department of the Treasury and Internal Revenue Service, Examples of Program-Related Investments, *Federal Register* 77:76 (April 19, 2012): 23429–23432. See also Richard L. Fox, "Private Foundations Get Expanded Program-Related Investment Options," *Estate Planning* 40:1 (January 2013): 23–28, and David A. Levitt and Robert A. Wesler, "Proposed Regulations Would Bring Program-Related Investments into the 21st Century," *Journal of Taxation* 117:2 (August 2010): 100–114.

10.   Lewis D. Solomon, "Microenterprise: Human Reconstruction in America's Inner Cities," *Harvard Journal of Law & Public Policy* 15:1 (Winter 1992): 191–221.

11.   Jon Zemke, "Thinking outside the bank," *Crain's Detroit Business* 27:34 (August 22, 2011): S27.

12.   Kiva Detroit, "What is Kiva Detroit" <www.Kiva.org/detroit> (August 5, 2011). See also Tom Walsh, "Microloans deserve praise," *Detroit Free Press*, June 29, 2011, C1, and *Chronicle of Philanthropy*, "Kiva Program Highlights Detroit Small Business," July 28, 2011, 15.

13.   Christina Rogers, "WSU's TechTown booming," *Detroit News*, February 13, 2010, B7; Nicquel Terry, "TechTown nurtures entrepreneurs," *Detroit Free Press*, August 9, 2009, B4; Nathan Hurst, "High-tech startups flourish at WSU site," *Detroit News*, May 9, 2009, A1. For background on Wayne State University, see Libby Sander, "A University in Detroit Pins New

Hopes on Old Buildings," *Chronicle of Higher Education* 55:5 (May 8, 2009): A13–A14.

In 2012, TechTown received a grant from The New Economy Initiative (NEI) to create the High Tech Accelerator, an inside business incubator, to get TechTown back to its original mission of incubating emerging tech companies. The NEI will also support companies inside the High Tech Accelerator with a new $5 million fund, the Capital Equity Fund, which will make equity investments of up to $250,000 in startups. Tom Henderson, "NEI crafts program to boost tech," *Crain's Detroit Business* 28:10 (March 5, 2012): 1.

14. Reginald Stuart, "Innovation Engine: Wayne State University's TechTown is helping revive Detroit's hard-hit economy," *Diverse: Issues in Higher Education* 29:1 (February 16, 2012): 14–15. In 2011, the NEI quietly came to the rescue of TechTown by providing $5.9 million grant which enabled the business incubator to pay off part of a mortgage and refinance the remainder. *Crain's Detroit Business*, "Rumblings," 27:37 (September 5, 2011): 30.

15. Wayne State University, Press Release, "Wayne State University Research and Technology Park marks grand opening of TechOne Building," April 16, 2004 <www.media.wayne.edu/2004/04/16> (December 7, 2011); "TechTown, run in Stakeholders" <www.techtownwsu.org/about/stakeholders> (June 8, 2012) and "Partners" <www.techtownwsu.org/about/partners> (June 8, 2012). See also David Jesse, "WSU incubator sets its sights on neighborhood's small businesses," *Detroit Free Press*, November 7, 2011, A1, and Michael V. Copeland, "Making Detroit High Tech," *Fortune* 161:3 (March 1, 2010): 29–30.

16. The statistics in this paragraph are from TechTown, Impact Report Update 2007–2011, n.d., n.p.

17. WSU, Press Release, "TechTown prepares Detroit expansion with 'TechTwo,'" February 14, 2010 <www.media.wayne.edu/report.php?id=7111> (June 28, 2012). See also Katherine Yung, "TechTwo takes shape," *Detroit Free Press*, January 18, 2011, C1, and Christina Rogers, "WSU's TechTown booming," *Detroit News*, February 13, 2010, B7.

18. WSU, Press Release, "800k Kresge grant supports expansion of TechTown's business incubator park," April 14, 2010 <www.media.wayne.edu/2010/04/800k-Kresge-grant-supports-expansion> (December 7, 2011).

19. Katherine Yung, "Loan to boost tech in Detroit," *Detroit Free Press*, October 5, 2010, C3.

20. WSU, Press Release, "The Blackstone Charitable Foundation invests $50m to support entrepreneurship globally," April 30, 2010 <www.media.wayne.edu/2010/04/30> (December 7, 2011). See also Tom Walsh, "Career launch effort starts," *Detroit Free Press*, April 30, 2010, A12.

21. Bizdom U, "FAQs,"< www.bizdom.com/faq> (September 12, 2011); "About the Program," <www.bizdom.com/program> (September 12, 2011); "Our Entrepreneurs Invest," <www.bizdom.com/program/entrepreneurers> (September 12, 2011); "Business Development and Planning," <www.bizdom.com/program/business-development-funding> (September 12, 2011). See also Sarah Schmid, "Bizdom U: Transforming Detroit's Brain Economy," October 31, 2011 <www.xconomy.com/detroit/2011/10/31> (May 29, 2012); Pamela Ryckman, "Fostering Entrepreneurs, and Trying to Revive a City,"

New York Times, June 24, 2010, B6; Jon Swartz, "Thanks to Bizdom U, Detroit Builds Entrepreneurs, Too," *USA Today*, April 20, 2009, B1; Jennifer Youssef, "Bizdom U grads set to go local," *Detroit News*, September 29, 2008, A8; Tom Walsh, "Entrepreneurs ready to get city's economy rolling," *Detroit Free Press*, July 31, 2008, 1; Jennifer Youssef, "A spark for startups," *Detroit News*, June 15, 2007, C1; Jennifer Youssef, "Bizdom U gets ideas off the ground," *Detroit News*, December 18, 2006, C1; Shenna Harrison, "Bizdom U Set to Teach Next Gen of Startups," *Crain's Detroit Business* 22:46 (November 13, 2006): 1.

22.   Detroit Regional Workforce Fund (DRWF), Addressing Detroit's Basic Skills Crisis, n.d., 2, 6, 7. See also Katherine Yung, "Detroit lacking services for job skills, study finds," *Detroit Free Press*, May 8, 2011, B1.

23.   DRWF, Addressing, 8–9.

24.   For an analysis of current federal workforce development efforts see Lewis D. Solomon, *Cycles of Poverty and Crime in America's Inner Cities* (New Brunswick, NJ: Transaction, 2012): 30–41, 51–54.

25.   Gordon Lafer, *The Job Training Charade* (Ithaca, NY: Cornell University, 2002): 116.

26.   Richard Florida, *The Rise of the Creative Class and How It's Transforming Work, Leisure, Community, and Everyday Life* (New York: Basic, 2002). See also Richard Florida, "People Who Can Rebuild a City," *New York Times*, July 26, 2002, A21. Critiques that the Creative Class provides false hope to cities, such as Detroit, in their revitalization efforts include Alec Macqillis, "The Ruse of the Creative Class," *American Prospect* 21:1 (January/February 2010): 12–16; Jamie Peck, "Struggling with the Creative Class," *International Journal of Urban and Regulatory Research* 29:4 (December 2005): 740–770; Steven Malanga, "The Curse of the Creative Class," *City Journal* 14:1 (Winter 2004): 36–35.

27.   Richard Florida, "The Rise of the Creative Class," *Washington Monthly* 34:5 (May 2005): 15–25.

28.   Florida, "The Rise," 8.

29.   See generally Rochelle Riley, "State of the Arts: Can an Infusion of Creators or Curators Drawn to the Affordable Space, Lead the Way?," *Ebony* 66:9 (July 2011): 108–09; Louis Aguilar, "Cool factor lures the young, artsy to Detroit," *Detroit News*, June 29, 2011, A1; Mark Stryker, "Can arts and culture save Detroit?," *Detroit Free Press*, April 3, 2011, E2; Patricia Montemurri, "The houses that art build," *Detroit Free Press*, December 27, 2010, A1; Melena Ryzik, "Wringing Art Out of the Rubble in Detroit," *New York Times*, August 4, 2010, C1; Rob Walker, "Art With Abandon," *New York Times Magazine*, July 11, 2010, 20.

30.   Rip Rapson, "Why Art Matters," April 10, 2011 <www.kresge.org/about-us/presidents-corner/art-x-detroit-why-art-matters> (December 7, 2011).

31.   Power House Productions, "Info" <www.powerhouseproject.com/index.php?/updates/info-statements> (November 30, 2011) and "Power House Productions Narrative" <www.powerhouseproject.com/index.php?/programs/future-projects> (November 30, 2011). See also Patricia Montemurri, "The houses" and Michael H. Hodges, "Visitors turn old houses into artwork," *Detroit News*, November 11, 2011, M14.

32.   David Whitford, "Factory of Dreams," *Fortune* 162:1 (July 5, 2010): 63–66.

33. Marney Rich Keenan, "Nourishing Detroit Soup," *Detroit News*, May 4, 2011, A2.

34. Zemke, "Thinking outside."

35. John Gallagher, "The arts aid business," *Detroit Free Press*, April 24, 2011, B1. See also James Heilbrun and Charles M. Gray, *The Economics of Art and Culture*, second edition (New York: Cambridge University, 2001), 336–359; Ann Markusen and David King, The Artistic Dividend: The Arts' Hidden Contribution to Regional Development, Arts Research Monitor 2:5 (November 2003); Neil Scott Kleiman with Robin Keegan et al., The Creative Engine: How Arts & Culture is Fueling Economic Growth in the New York City Neighborhoods, Center for an Urban Future, November 2002; John M. Eger, The Creative Community: Forging Links between Art Culture Commerce & Community, California Institute for Smart Communities, San Diego State University, 2003.

   For an analysis of how economic impact studies misrepresent the benefits of nonprofit arts and cultural organizations, see Arthur H. Sterngold, "Do Economic Impact Studies Misrepresent the Benefits of Arts and Cultural Organizations?," *Journal of Arts Management, Law & Society* 34:3 (Fall 2004): 166–187.

   For a discussion of the various types of economic impacts and the methodologies used to quantify the benefits of artists to an economy, see Bruce A. Seaman, "Economic Impact of the Arts," in *A Handbook of Cultural Economics*, ed. Ruth Towse (Northampton, MA: Edward Elgar, 2003): 224–225.

36. The Kresge Foundation (Kresge), Press Release, "2012 Kresge Artist Fellows highlight culturally 'rich environment' of Metro Detroit: $600,000 in fellowships to Detroit area literary and performing artists," June 28, 2012 <www.kresge.org/news/kresge-artist-fellows-highlight-culturally> (July 2, 2012); Kresge, Press Release, "The Kresge Foundation awards $300,000 in fellowships to Detroit area visual artists: Twelve $25,000 prizes are awarded," June 27, 2011 <www.kresge.org/news/kresge-foundation-awards-300000-fellowships> (December 7, 2011); Kresge, Press Release, "The Kresge Foundation awards $450,000 in fellowships to Detroit area literacy and performing artists: 18 artists receive $25,000 each," June 29, 2010 <www.kresge.org/news/kresge-foundation-awards-450000-fellowships> (December 8, 2011); Kresge, Press Release, "Kresge Foundation awards $450,000 in fellowships to Detroit area visual artists: 18 artists receive $25,000 each," June 29, 2009 <www.kresge.org/news/kresge-foundation-awards-450000-fellowships> (December 8, 2011). See also, B. J. Hammerstein, "Kresge Foundation names 2012 recipients of $25,000 grants," *Detroit Free Press*, June 28, 2012, A11; Susan Whitall, "24 Metro Detroiters win Kresge grants," *Detroit News*, June 28, 2012, D4; Mark Stryker, "Kresge artists get $25 grand," *Detroit Free Press*, June 29, 2011, D1; Michael H. Hodges, "Kresge names grant recipients," *Detroit News*, June 30, 2010, A9; Mark Stryker, "Kresge gives local visual artists $25,000 each," *Detroit Free Press*, June 30, 2009, A5.

37. Kresge, Press Release, "Kresge sponsors Art X Detroit: A new Detroit arts experience in Midtown, April 6–10, 2011" <www.kresge.org/news/kresge-sponsors-art-x-detroit-new-detroit-arts-experience> (December 7, 2011) and Kresge, Press Release, "Kresge Foundation Launches Art X Detroit to Celebrate Artistic Excellence and the City's Creative Spirit,

April 6–10, 2011" <www.artxdetroit.com/press> (December 7, 2011). See also, Gallagher, "The arts aid business;" Mark Stryker, "Art X Detroit trumpets local culture, celebrates big ideas," *Detroit Free Press*, April 3, 2011, A1; Brian McCollum, "Kresge Foundation to fund new Detroit arts fest," *Detroit Free Press*, February 10, 2011, D1.

38. Detroit Creative Corridor Center (DC3), "Our Purpose" <www.detroitcreativecorridorcenter.com/about/our-story> (May 29, 2012) and "Governance" <www.detroitcreativecorridorcenter.com.about/governance> (May 29, 2012). For the benefits of art-based business incubators, see Rhonda Phillips, "Artful business: Using the arts for community economic development," *Community Development Journal* 39:2 (April 2004): 112–122, at 114–116.

39. DC3, "Business Acceleration: Creative Ventures Update," October 25, 2011 <www.detroitcreativecorridorcenter.com/2011/10/25/updates> (November 22, 2011) and "Accelerator Studio," July 25, 2011 <www.detroitcreativecorridorcenter.com/2011/07/27/accelerator-studio> (November 22, 2011). See also Jaclyn Trop, "City's creative economy gets jump-start," *Detroit News*, July 12, 2011, A10, and Tom Walsh, "Creative corridor not so kooky now," *Detroit Free Press*, July 10, 2011, B1.

40. Mark J. Stern and Susan C. Seifert, "From Creative Economy to Creative Society," Social Impact of the Arts Project, January 2008.

41. Ibid., 3.

42. See Phil Hubbard and Tim Hall, "The Entrepreneurial City and the 'New Urban Politics,'" in *The Entrepreneurial City: Geographies of Politics, Regime and Representation*, eds. Tim Hall and Phil Hubbard (Chichester, West Sussex, England: John Wiley, 1998).

IV

A Vision of and Obstacles to the Creation of an Alternative Political Economy Sector

In the twenty-first century, Detroiters may come to realize that neither a shrunken public sector nor burgeoning for-profit entities will provide the complete solutions to the array of the city's problems discussed in chapter 1. Rather than looking to Washington, DC, Lansing, or Dan Gilbert, among other business executives, residents may turn inward and seek to build more self-sufficient, more sustainable community-based institutions—beginning with food, and going on to form business cooperatives and implement a local currency, perhaps called Detroit Dollars. The benefits of and the obstacles to the creation of a parallel, alternative political economy sector are examined in chapter 8.

8

The Potential Role of an Alternative Political Economy Sector in Detroit's Revival

Focusing on development in terms of the quality of life, residents may become more cognizant of the need to create a new, locally based, more self-reliant system,[1] making use of two key resources: vacant land and underutilized human capabilities. Building on existing neighborhood institutions and establishing new ones, Detroiters may come to realize that their material needs, as opposed to their wants, are much simpler than they previously thought. A community-driven approach could serve residents' basic needs: food, shelter, health care, clothing, and education. Residents could create a less consumption-oriented lifestyle and a more self-sufficient pattern centered on the local production and distribution of goods and services. They could create a model of urban sustainability, far less reliant on the public sector, thereby upsetting the prevalent, nearly eighty-year-old pattern.

This chapter begins by examining the significant amount of vacant land in Detroit and its possible uses. The existence of numerous urban gardens and their nutritional advantages are considered.

Next, the realities of achieving greater self-sufficiency in food are discussed. The economic, environmental, and social benefits of an alternative political economy, and the obstacles to implementing such a sector, are reviewed. The chapter concludes with a brief examination of a local currency system.

Despite the rationality of the vision sketched in this chapter, long odds exist with respect to Detroiters implementing a parallel, alternative political economy sector. Apart from the various obstacles—practical, legal, cultural, and psychological—analyzed in this chapter. It is extremely difficult to turn back from both the entitlement state and the American dream of a well-paying job, a nice house and good car, and a comfortable retirement.

Vacant Land: A Significant Resource

The alternative political economy sector rests on the constructive use of Detroit's vast, untapped resources: vacant land and its unskilled workforce. As developed in chapter 1, vacant land and abandoned structures that result in blighted blocks fill huge sections of Detroit. Some 40 square miles out of the city's 139 square miles consist of vacant land.[2] According to the best estimates,[3] citywide there are slightly more than 100,000 (100,719) vacant parcels in public and private hands, with 41,864 lots of publicly owned vacant land and 4,106 tracts of improved publicly owned land. Residential properties (37,960 or 87 percent) dominate the public portfolio, with 3,299 (7 percent) commercial, retail, and office properties and 2,974 (6 percent) industrial properties. Of the 47,203 parcels in public ownership, including those not mapped, the Detroit Planning and Development Department controls the vast majority (85 percent or 38,461 parcels), with the Michigan Land Bank Fast Track Authority holding the rest. The publicly owned lots equal about 12,000 acres, or some 13 percent of the city's entire land mass, with 96 percent of these parcels under 10,000 square feet and most about .15 acres (6,530 square feet) in size.

Public land ownership adds little, if any, value in terms of jobs and property taxes. Rather, it drains public resources and often increases the blight in neighborhoods. Detroit lacks the financial resources to maintain these vacant publicly owned structures up to its own building-code standards. Vacant properties also impose increased public-safety costs related to code-enforcement, police, and fire services.[4] Abandoned structures, especially those near public schools, pose special problems, particularly in terms of drug dealing and other criminal activities.

Demolition of abandoned buildings continues, with Mayor Bing promising to knock down a total of about 10,000 homes by the end of his term in 2013.[5] Although largely funded by the federal Neighborhood Stabilization Program,[6] which provides grants for various approaches to try to resuscitate ailing real estate markets tailored to local conditions, Detroit has insufficient financial resources to address its 33,000 dangerous buildings—open to trespassers, fire damaged, or structurally unsafe, as of early 2012. Costing some $5,000 to $8,000 to demolish and clear a house, including asbestos removal and utility shutoffs, by April 2012, Bing had spent more than $20 million in mostly federal (with some state) funds to demolish 4,205 structures. He needs another $25 million to knock down and clear an additional 5,800 structures.[7] Even if funds are available, under the city's thirty-six-step process, it takes about 120 days to complete the demolition of municipal-owned properties.[8]

Beyond the need to place municipal finances on a sound course (discussed in chapter 3), turn around failing public schools (analyzed in chapter 5), and reduce unemployment through workforce development and private-sector economic growth (chapters 6 and 7), what to do with the existing vacant land and future open spaces resulting from demolitions represents an unresolved but pressing public-policy problem. Land use and its management, especially with respect to publicly owned parcels, represents a complex matter in view of Detroit's constrained financial resources. Even envisioning some future forms of homesteading, it seems highly unlikely that demand will exist in coming decades (or even during this century) for rebuilding single-family, detached residences or even multi-family dwellings across the amount of available, publicly held land in Detroit.

Other more practical land-use possibilities exist, including various "green" initiatives.[9] Open land enables the replenishing of the watershed, by allowing rain to soak into the soil rather than running off into the city's combined storm water–sewer system. Thus, green spaces would help Detroit manage its current storm-water problem, thereby lessening the need to renovate its sewer system or rebuild new wastewater facilities. Open land also creates recreational opportunities. It facilitates the absorption of carbon dioxide and lessens the impact of urban heat islands that raise temperatures. Apart from removing more abandoned homes and buildings, thereby adding to the number of existing vacant lots, and then reforesting the dead land zones, creating large networks of parks (or greenways through the open spaces to link neighborhoods), or simply letting barren areas revert to nature—another approach would focus on converting vacant land (and even whole neighborhoods) into urban farms. The thousands of acres of empty, publicly held land make Detroit ripe for the creation of a parallel, alternative political economy sector built around urban agriculture and focused on a greater degree of local self-sufficiency. However, significant practical and legal obstacles interfere with the implementation of this vision.

Gardens in Detroit

Today, urban gardens have sprouted on empty lots and the abandoned open spaces. At present, more than 1,200 community, market, institutional, and household gardens have taken root in Detroit.[10] Gardeners grow more than seventy varieties of fruits and vegetables in 328 community, 39 market, 63 school, and 804 family gardens. In addition to planting in their backyards, residents have claimed abandoned lots adjacent to their homes or created larger gardens from several contiguous vacant lots.

Community gardens, consisting of open, urban spaces shared by residents to grow food, have flourished. Operating these urban gardens, community-based organizations have helped residents transform barren neighborhoods into fertile small plots to help feed impoverished families and beautify blighted blocks. They have provided strong, effective leadership in neighborhoods throughout the city. For example, the Georgia Street Community Collective, which operates three community gardens, supplies its neighborhood with fresh fruits and vegetables. It also provides education and leadership skills to area youth and supports a community center/library.[11]

Building on their agricultural activities, neighborhood-focused leadership has organized and implemented the labor-intensive efforts to rebuild and sustain areas within Detroit. The Detroit Black Community Food Security Network, for example, not only meets local residents' needs for fresh produce but also helps build a vibrant community using vacant land, thereby transforming the social, economic, and physical environment. Its urban farm, D-Town, includes organic vegetable plots, two beehives, a composting operation, and a hoop house (an unheated structure with a roof and sides made largely out of transparent or translucent material, not glass) for year-round food production. It has organized a food cooperative buying club and partners with three local African-centered schools to introduce elementary students to agriculture. The network disseminates information about healthy foods and lifestyles. Serving as a tangible example of self-reliance and accomplishment through collective efforts, it also has a successful record of political activism. The network was instrumental in the Detroit City Council adopting a Food Security Policy and implementing a Food Policy Council in 2008 and 2009, respectively.[12]

In sum, a significant role exists for neighborhood-based institutions. They have combated some of Detroit's urban woes, including hunger and a proliferation of vacant lots and derelict, crime-ridden, abandoned homes. They have made residents healthier by building local foods systems, ones that produce and distribute affordable, nutritious fruits and vegetables not only to organizational participants but also to others.

The Nutritional Benefits of Community Gardens

The nutritional benefits of community gardens are numerous.[13] Increasing healthy food options helps reduce hunger experienced by impoverished Detroit residents. If expanded, these gardens could supply low-income individuals and families with fresh, healthful, locally grown produce in the so-called "food deserts,"[14] areas of Detroit, lacking supermarkets and other retail outlets offering affordable, fresh fruits and vegetables. Improved access to nutritional food grown in community gardens, especially on abandoned lots, and distributed through neighborhood farmers' markets could improve human health by lessening the current obesity epidemic.[15]

In concept, a relationship exists between the mode of food distribution and high obesity rates, especially in America's inner cities, such as many areas of Detroit. Low-income urban areas suffer from high rates of diet-related diseases, such as diabetes and heart disease, resulting, in part, from an abundance of processed, high-calorie foods of low-nutritional quality. Eating more fresh fruits and vegetables, coupled with more physical activity, could help reduce the incidence of these diet-related illnesses. However, empirical studies indicate that improved proximity to healthy foods does not lead to better health outcomes.[16]

Greater Self-Sufficiency in Food: The Realities

Significant levels of self-sufficiency in Detroit, beginning with food, are possible. Studies indicate that agriculture, whether in the form of gardens, greenhouses, or vertical farms, could supply local residents, under various scenarios, with from 31 percent of their fresh vegetables and 17 percent of their fresh, nontropical fruit to potentially 76 percent of their fresh vegetables and 42 percent of their fresh, nontropical fruit.[17] Tilling a relatively modest number of acres could also generate thousands of jobs.

In painting this rosy scenario of locally producing food for community needs, using available land and labor, it is important to note that many of the risks of urban agriculture are solvable.[18] After surmounting the initial site-cleaning costs, which can be prohibitive and must be investigated, issues of urban soil quality exist, particularly with respect to former factory sites. Although soil contamination with heavy metals, such as lead, pose human health problems, ways exist to eliminate the risks of lead and other forms of debasement, for example, through chemical stabilization procedures. Or, urban farms could use hydroponics as a growing technique. Healthy soil could be brought in with raised beds created on top of the contaminated soil. After hammering boards together to make a raised bed, good dirt could be made from a compost of decaying leaves, coffee grounds, and the cheap new soil.

Looking to the future, selectively growing crops that have a lower propensity to accumulate lead, among other hazardous metals, offers promise. Because the risk of lead in the soil comes from the metal washing off the sides of housing, among other structures, during rainfall and from auto and industrial emissions, urban farmers could use an ecologically sound method of food cultivation to keep the soil covered, thereby minimizing dust pollution. In sum, apart from the contamination problem, which can be addressed, although the soil quality on vacant lots in residential areas is variable, generally speaking it is acceptable for growing fruits and vegetables in cities such as Detroit.[19]

The Benefits of an Alternative, More Self-Reliant Political Economy Sector

A more self-reliant urban food system would not only help repair the nutritional gaps in the existing conventional food network in Detroit, particularly for the unemployed and the working poor, but also offer numerous other benefits: economic, environmental, and social.[20]

Economic Benefits. A community-based food system would support the creation and enhancement of food-related productive economic opportunities for Detroiters. It would offer meaningful work for the chronically unemployed, particularly those who did not graduate from high school, enabling them to be less dependent on public sector-entitlements. Unskilled residents with some training could do much of the required work. Although hand-tended agriculture is hard work, characterized by hot, dusty field labor, it teaches job skills and builds an enhanced sense of personal responsibility. It also offers an opportunity for people, even those who initially lack farm skills, to be useful, thereby helping restore their self-esteem.

Many African Americans came north to Detroit, among other cities, to leave jobs in agriculture, particularly sharecropping, behind and pursue opportunities in manufacturing. Thus, it is unclear whether large numbers of blacks will look favorably on farm work, and see it as a means of empowerment and hope.

Other obstacles include difficulties related to marketing and distribution. However, Detroit has a significant asset: its Eastern Market (mentioned in chapter 2), a major food processing and distribution center.

Also, a locally based, urban food system could generate entrepreneurial opportunities, including the creation of worker-owned cooperatives,[21] to handle food processing and distribution as well as food waste management. In a community-owned cannery, for example, people could preserve produce for subsequent sale. These spin-off endeavors would likely lead to additional employment gains.

Beyond the food system, small worker-owned enterprises could produce other goods and services, such as clothing, for the local market. In these smaller, less-complex economic organizations, ownership would not be separated from personal involvement in the entities. The employees, as owners, would experience increased responsibilities and participation in decision making. Because the employee-members would have a greater stake in a venture, they probably would be more motivated to help make the business succeed.

These business cooperatives would use the market mechanism to gather information about consumer preferences and allocate resources in accordance with preferences, hopefully meeting basic human needs. Cooperatives may also permit the development of various services— such as child care, care for the elderly, and transportation—more effectively, with more flexibility, and at lower cost. When coupled with a local currency, discussed later in this chapter, these community businesses would help strengthen Detroit's economy by reducing the current economic leakages that flow outside the city. More funds would be retained locally.

Environmental Benefits. Increased local food production would encourage the use of limited resources in a more efficient, sustainable manner. It would reduce the problems associated with storm-water run-off, resulting in sewage that flows into local rivers, by redirecting rainwater to the gardens, and thus, through the landscape, thereby reducing the cost of waste-water management. Collecting urban food and yard waste could produce compost for use as a nutrient source. Increased self-reliance in food, as well as other goods, would minimize the energy use involved in transporting produce, among other items, thereby minimizing air pollution and possibly encouraging the use of renewable energy resources.

Rapid obsolescence and replacement with new goods characterize our current throwaway economy. Neighborhoods could form repair groups for individuals to pool their skills and labor for several hours a month to fix broken lamps and vacuum cleaners, among other items, and mend old clothes.[22] Beyond an environmental mission, these centers could serve a social objective, by creating new places for people to meet.

Social Benefits. Decentralized, smaller scale institutions would, more generally, enhance a sense of community.[23] Strengthening neighborhood ties would likely reduce drug dealing and other forms of criminality. By facilitating local decision making, each person would hopefully see the need to take a more active role in a society where his or her actions would have enhanced meaning and impact.

In sum, building on community-based food system activities such as production, processing, and distribution would enable neighborhoods in Detroit to strive to achieve broader goals, including a different type of economic vitality, through a sustainable alternative to consumerism—providing increased labor-intensive employment, and even taking over social service functions currently performed by the public sector. For example, community-based entities such as mutual-aid societies, private voluntary-membership associations of individuals, could sponsor health care clinics[24] offering preventive, primary care. As neighborhood groups assume tasks once monopolized by the public sector, more functions could move downstream to the neighborhoods and more services could be tailored to meet community needs.

Obstacles to Building an Alternative Political Economy Sector

The vision of community-based farms, cooperative businesses, and taking more services away from the public sector encounters three significant obstacles: one practical and two legal.

Practical Obstacles. The business end of a community-based economic sector, characterized by a high degree of local self-sufficiency, requires a substantial time commitment by participants, not merely a few hours a week or a month, at low pay. Worker-owned entities also require start-up and operational capital. Using noncapital-intensive (capital-saving) techniques could partially reduce the financing needs that traditionally have retarded the development of business cooperatives. As with for-profit start-ups, foundations (using the program-related investment strategy discussed in chapter 7) and wealthy individuals could assist in funding the establishment and continued operation of community gardens as well as food and other businesses.

Two Legal Obstacles. Two legal obstacles interfere with building an alternative political economy sector. First, leasing or acquiring publicly owned land in Detroit is not a simple matter. At present, individuals or groups can adopt a plot of city-owned land to start an urban farm. No fee is required, only the completion of a Detroit Planning and Development Department application.[25] If approved, the department issues an annual permit for use from January to December each year. Use of the land for more than one year requires annual reapplication. Lacking ownership, a community garden faces the possibility, perhaps remote, of being forced to move. As an alternative, the city should offer urban farms a more permanent tenure, for example, a long-term lease of ten years.

To make land tenure even more secure, Detroit must make it easier to buy tax-reverted land for agricultural use by simplifying its often intractable bureaucracy and removing the city council's approval of each city-owned land sale.[26] These both currently slow the disposition process. With the city and the Michigan Land Bank Fast Track Authority controlling so much of Detroit's unoccupied land, putting vacant lots to productive use would not only increase the tax base but also raise property values.[27] Consideration should also be given to providing incentives, such as reduced tax assessments, for properties with significant agricultural uses. Land sold for farm purposes should, however, revert back to public ownership (or be subject to higher assessments), if not used for agriculture within a specified time period.

In contemplating the city's return of a large portion of its presently unused, untaxed land to private hands, Detroit must create a comprehensive database of all the jurisdiction's publicly owned properties. Whether it sells land to individuals, community groups, or nonprofit land trusts (which, in turn, lease parcels to others for agricultural uses), Detroit must offer purchasers clear title, not a quit-claim deed that provides no assurance that title is not clouded with various liens and/or prior owners' rights.

Hopefully, in the near term, Detroit will resolve what to do with its publicly owned vacant land. Even in the absence of long-term leases or a turnover of public land, community and backyard gardens will continue to flourish.

Second, a need exists for Detroit zoning and land-use policies to support urban food production. At present, while not prohibiting farming, the Detroit zoning ordinance does not support urban agriculture as a land use. Because the city's zoning code does not currently recognize agriculture as a permitted use, food-growing efforts currently exist on the gray side of the law. These efforts represent a nonconforming, if not illegal, use theoretically subject to fines. To date, the city has chosen not to enforce its zoning law because the non-permitted gardens represent a "good and beneficial use."[28]

If Detroit knows that an individual or a group is engaging in a non-permitted use on land that he, she, or it owns and does nothing, such a use is subject to the doctrine of laches. Specifically, an unreasonable delay by the city in pursuing a right or a claim may constitute a waiver of such right or claim. Thus, a need exists to amend Detroit's zoning ordinance to cover urban agriculture.

One significant obstacle to revising the city's zoning code seems to have been removed. In December 2011, amendments to the state farm regulations aimed at promoting commercial agriculture effectively exempted Detroit, among other large Michigan cities, from a provision of the state's Right to Farm Act.[29]

Enacted in 1981, the act empowers farmers in rural and suburban areas by allowing them to choose their own crops and types of agriculture, and protects them from suburban sprawl encroachments, specifically subdivision developers gobbling up farmland. The act renders farmers immune from nuisance suits filed by neighbors, objecting to the ordinary noises and aromas of farming, that otherwise would threaten farms.

Prior to the 2011 regulatory amendment, the act also exempted farms from local zoning codes, provided they complied with the standards set by Michigan Generally Accepted Agricultural and Management Practices (MGAAMP) designed to protect farms against nuisance suits, among other goals. Thus, prior to the amendment, if the Detroit zoning ordinance recognized agriculture as a permitted use, under the Michigan Right to Farm Act any attempt by the city to set different standards from the MGAAMP would have been invalid. As amended, however, the Michigan Department of Agriculture & Rural Development regulations now exempt Detroit from the state's Right to Farm Act, provided its zoning code "designates existing agricultural operations present prior to the ordinance's adoption as legal nonconforming uses as identified by the Right to Farm Act for purposes of scale and type of agricultural use."[30] Without the exemption, Detroit would have been reluctant to permit agriculture, particularly the commercial raising of livestock, out of concerns that it would be unable to control various nuisance factors, among other items, under the act. Now, seemingly Detroit can regulate urban agriculture, including the commercial production of food products, by its zoning ordinance and thereby protect neighborhood residents. The regulatory amendment represents a first step, hopefully followed by the Michigan legislature specifically exempting Detroit from the Right to Farm Act. At present, it is uncertain whether the legislature will amend the act to permit local control of urban agriculture.

Building on the regulatory amendment, Detroit needs to specify the zoning rules for urban agriculture—including the who, what, where, and how of permitted farm activities. Detroit ought to allow community and backyard gardens, even for-profit commercial farms such as Hantz Farms,[31] to operate in the city, but in a manner respectful of neighbors. A comprehensive approach requires the resolution of numerous questions. Will all types of agriculture be allowed in commercial and industrial districts, or will only rooftop and vertical gardens be permitted? What types of agricultural use will be permitted in residential areas? What kinds of chemicals can be used? What about farm animals, such as livestock and chickens, and bee-keeping (apiculture)?[32] A need also exists for specifying soil-testing standards and for a process to safeguard food cultivation grown on remediated soil, especially on former industrial or other contaminated sites.

Creating a Local Currency System

With significant levels of local self-reliance, beginning with food, even a remote possibility, consideration should be given to implementing a local currency, perhaps called Detroit Dollars, to parallel US dollars.[33] Detroit Dollars would help residents on a sensible path to renewal by augmenting the current lack of US dollars. Models, such as Ithaca Hours, exist of long-standing, successful local currency systems.[34]

Detroit Dollars, as an example of an alternative currency, would represent labor that produces goods and services, hopefully, meeting basic human needs. Each Detroit Dollar could be valued at ten (or twenty) dollars per hour of labor. Businesses, professionals, and others could request multiple Detroit Dollars per hour of work performed.

Local finance, based on an alternative currency, would strengthen Detroit's economy in a number of aspects and help build a new economic sector. Implementation of a local currency system would likely generate employment gains through job creation, and enhance for-profit and community-based entrepreneurial opportunities in food and nonfood sectors, such as clothing. By stimulating the sale of items not currently produced in the city, Detroit Dollars would also promote a greater degree of local self-reliance.

Detroit has numerous willing, but unskilled, workers; some of them, as noted in chapter 1, have dropped out of the workforce, in part, because individuals and businesses lack the funds to hire them. Similar to land, labor in Detroit represents an abundant but untapped resource. By honoring skills neglected by the formal political economy based on US dollars, an alternative currency would enable individuals (and businesses) to monetize their labor and bring them into the new economic sector, thereby serving as a path to revitalization.

Detroit Dollars, which could only be used in the city, would promote local commerce and facilitate the retention of funds in the community. They would stimulate new enterprises, including community-based gardens and business cooperatives, as well as for-profit start-ups and existing local for-profit firms. They would encourage innovation because individuals and groups would think about different goods or services they could offer participants in the system. By expanding the market for locally produced and distributed goods and services, the alternative currency would, as noted, increase the employment of Detroit residents. With individuals and entities patronizing each other and spending the local currency within the city, more income generated in Detroit would remain there, further stimulating the formal and the new parallel-economic sector. The retention of more funds would likely facilitate the financing of additional small-scale entities. An alternative currency would help revive the formal economy by enlarging Detroit's income and sales tax revenues. It would also assist in linking neighborhood associations to one another so as to promote cooperation as well as resource- and solution-sharing among them and strengthen civil society by heightening a sense of closeness among neighbors. Most importantly, a local currency would help link consumers to producers in a mutual effort to build an alternative political economy sector, one paralleling the existing public and for-profit private sectors.

A local currency system is legal provided it is not: first, issued by a state or any part of state government;[35] and second, coinage or a fractional paper currency of less than one dollar.[36] Thus, a nonpublic-sector entity, such as a locally based, democratically organized nonprofit entity, could issue an alternative currency in paper or electronic format (the latter with computer-tallied credits and debits) in amounts of one dollar or more provided, under the federal anti-counterfeit provisions, it is not similar to US currency.[37]

A nonprofit organization, funded by foundations and wealthy individuals, could issue Detroit Dollars. Although legal in paper and electronic format, with paper the way to proceed initially as a symbol, a cultural artifact, a local currency system requires constant monitoring with an eye for calibrating the issuance to balance circulation and prevent devaluation. In addition to an administrative body and staff, the system also requires funding for "networkers" to contact enterprises and residents to promote, facilitate, and troubleshoot the system. The need to print a paper currency so that it cannot be counterfeited represents another cost consideration.

Notes

1. For building of self-sufficient communities, see generally Michael H. Schuman, *Going Local: Creating Self-Reliant Communities in a Global Age* (New York: Free Press, 1998) and Lyle Estill, *Small Is Possible: Life in A Local Economy* (Gabriola Island, British Columbia, Canada: New Society Publishers, 2008). See also Olga Bonfiglio, "Delicious in Detroit," *Planning* 75:8 (August–September 2009): 32–37.

2. Detroit Works Project (DWP), Where Will People Live, Vacant Land Area is Overwhelming, n.d., n.p.

3. The statistics in this paragraph are from DWP, Phase One: Research and Priorities: Policy Audit Topic: Public Land Disposition Policies and Procedures, December 22, 2010, 3.4; Skidmore, Owings & Merrill LLP, Phase One: Research and Priorities: Policy Audit Topic: Land Use and Urban Form, DWP, December 17, 2000, 2.5 (City of Detroit Vacancy); DWP, "Opportunities to Reuse Publicly Owned Land," n.d., n.p. See also, *Detroit Free Press*, "Detroit is missing out by hoarding its land," April 1, 2012, A21; Christine MacDonald, "Vacant houses stoke city woes," *Detroit News*, December 26, 2011, A3; Suzette Hackney, "Detroit won't be reshaped easily," *Detroit Free Press*, April 6, 2011, A3; John Gallagher, *Reimagining Detroit: Opportunities for Redefining an American City* (Detroit: Wayne State University, 2010), 66.

4. US General Accountability Office (GAO), Vacant Properties: Growing Number Increases Communities' Costs and Challenges, November 2011, GAO-12-34, 42–43.

5. DWP, Phase One: Research and Priorities: Policy Audit Topic: Neighborhood, Community Development & Housing, December 17, 2010, 3.4 (Initiatives: Land: Demolition).

6. To date, Congress has allocated some $6.13 billion to the Neighborhood Stabilization Program through the following: the Emergency Assistance for the Redevelopment of Abandoned and Foreclosed Homes, Title III of the Housing and Economic Recovery Act of 2008, Public Law 110-289 ($3.2 billion allocation); Community Development Fund, part of the American Recovery and Reinvestment Act of 2009, Public Law 111-51 ($1.93 billion

allocation); Section 1497 of the Dodd-Frank Wall Street Reform and Consumer Protection Act, Public Law 111-203 ($1 billion allocation). As to the use of Neighborhood Stabilization Program funds, see Karla Henderson, "Detroit is putting all HUD funding to good use," *Detroit Free Press,* June 21, 2012, A14, and Todd Spangler, "Detroit, other Michigan cities must rush to spend $224M in housing aid or give it back," *Detroit Free Press,* June 3, 2012, A1.

7.   Chasity Pratt Dawsey and Kristi Tanner, "Too much blight, not enough cash," *Detroit Free Press,* April 15, 2012, A12, and MacDonald, "Vacant houses;" US GAO, Vacant Properties, 39, 42. But see Steve Neavling, "20m to demolish Detroit's burnt-out houses just sits there," *Detroit Free Press,* February 14, 2012, A1. Under a program announced in August 2012, the state plans to use some $10 million of Michigan's $97 million payout from a national mortgage-settlement fund to help demolish houses that surround nine schools in three of Detroit's deteriorating communities, thereby making school routes safer. Megha Satyanarayana, "1OM plan to make school routes safer," *Detroit Free Press,* August 3, 2012 <LexisNexis>; Matthew Dolan, "State to Unveil Detroit Demolition Plan," *Wall Street Journal,* August 2, 2012, A3; Megha Satyanarayana and Dawson Bell, "Snyder hopes to flatten city eyesores," *Detroit Free Press,* July 14, 2012, A1; Karen Bouffard, "State to target blighted Detroit neighborhoods," *Detroit News,* July 14, 2012, A1. The Pathways to Prosperity pilot program aims to make schools the hub of the community. Detroit Public Schools, Press Release, "Nine Detroit Schools the focus of a new intensive local, city, county, state collaborative effort to stabilize communities making schools their neighborhood hubs," August 2, 2012. See also Steve Pardo, "Project to boost neighborhoods," *Detroit News,* August 2, 2012, A6.

8.   Kristi Tanner, "Getting blight torn down no easy task," *Detroit Free Press,* April 15, 2012, A11.

9.   For a discussion of land-use possibilities, see Alan Mallach, "Depopulation, Market Collapse and Property Abandonment: Surplus Land and Buildings in Legacy Cities," in *Rebuilding America's Legacy Cities: New Directions for the Industrial Heartland,* ed. Alan Mallach (New York: American Assembly, 2012), 103–106 and Terry Schwarz, "Re-Thinking the Places in Between: Stabilization, Regeneration, and Reuse," in *Rebuilding America's Legacy Cities,* 172–173, 175–180.

10.   Kami Pothukuchi, The Detroit Food System Report 2009–2010, Detroit Food Policy Council, May 15, 2011, 59. For background on small-scale, local farming see Kirk Johnson, "Small Farmers Creating a New Business Model as Agriculture Goes Local," *New York Times,* July 2, 2012, A7.

11.   Georgia Street Community Collective, "About Us" <www.georgiastreetcc.com> (July 10, 2012). See also Detroit Food System Report 2009–2010, 60; David Josar, "Nature nurtured in Detroit's urban gardens," *Detroit News,* April 24, 2009, A8; Alex Altman, "Detroit Tries to Get on a Road to Renewal," *Time* 173:13 (March 26, 2009):40–45. For a list of Detroit urban agricultural initiatives and food system workforce/entrepreneurship developments, see Detroit Food System Report 2009–2010, 59–60, 64–66.

12.   Detroit Black Community Food Security Network, "Statement of Purpose" <www.detroitblackfoodsecurity.org/about.html> (November 18, 2011).

See also Monica M. While, "D-Town Farm: African American Resistance to Food Insecurity and the Transformation of Detroit," *Environmental Practice* 13:4 (December 2011): 406–417; Detroit Food System Report 2009–2010, 17–18; Tom Philpott, "Three projects that are watering Detroit's 'food desert,'" *Grist: Feeding the City,* September 11, 2010 <www.grist.org/article> (May 25, 2012). See generally, A City of Detroit Food Security Policy, "Creating a Food Secure Detroit" <www.detroitblackfoodsecurity.org/policy.html> (November 18, 2011) and Detroit Food Policy Council <www.detroitfoodpolicycouncil.net> (December 13, 2011). For background on food policy councils, see Kimberley Hodgson, Marcia Caton Campbell, Martin Bailkey, Urban Agriculture: Growing Healthy, Sustainable Places, American Planning Association, Planning Advisory Service, Report Number 563, 2011, 38–39.

13. See, e.g., Kate H. Brown and Andrew L. Jameton, "Public Health Implications of Urban Agriculture," *Journal of Public Health Policy* 21:1 (2000): 20–39. Hodgson, Campbell, Bailkey, Urban Agriculture, 20–21, summarize the healthy, social, economic, and environmental benefits of urban agriculture. See also Anne C. Bellows, Katherine Brown, Jac Smit, Health Benefits of Urban Agriculture, Community Food Security Coalition, n.d., and Jerry Kaufman and Martin Bailkey, Farming Inside Cities: Entrepreneurial Urban Agriculture in the United States, Lincoln Institute of Land Policy Working Paper, WP00JK1, 2000.

14. Shannon N. Zenk et al., "Fruit and Vegetable Access Differs by Community Racial Composition and Socioeconomic Position in Detroit, Michigan," *Ethnicity & Disease* 16:1 (Winter 2006): 275–280, concluded that the mean quality of fresh produce was significantly lower in a predominately African American, low-socioeconomic position community than in a racially heterogeneous, middle socioeconomic position community. See also Shannon N. Zenk et al., "Neighborhood Racial Composition, Neighborhood Poverty and the Spatial Accessibility of Supermarkets in Metropolitan Detroit," *American Journal of Public Health* 95:4 (April 2005): 660–667; Shannon N. Zenk et al., "Fruit and Vegetable Intake in African Americans: Income and Store Characteristics," *American Journal of Preventive Medicine* 29:1 (July 2005): 1–9; Shannon Nicole Zenk, Neighborhood Racial Composition, Neighborhood Poverty, and Food Access in Metropolitan Detroit: Geographic Information Systems and Spatial Analysis, Ph.D. Dissertation, University of Michigan, 2004, <ProQuest Dissertations and Theses>; Amy J. Schultz et al., "Racial and Spatial Relations as Fundamental Determinants of Health in Detroit," *Milbank Quarterly* 80:4 (December 2002): 277–707; Detroit Food System Report 2009–10, 30–32. According to one survey, Mari Gallagher Research & Consulting Group, Examining the Impact of Food Deserts on Public Health in Detroit, 2007, 80 percent of Detroit's residents must purchase their food at more than 1,000 fringe food retailers, such as liquor and convenience stores, and gas stations. A review article, Julie Beaulac, Elizabeth Kristjansson, Steven Cummings, "A Systematic Review of Feed **(Food?)** Deserts, 1996–2007," *Preventing Chronic Disease* 6:3 (July 2009): x–x, found clear evidence for disparities in food access in the United States by income and race. See also Tamara Dubowitz et al., "Neighborhood socioeconomic status and fruit and vegetable intake among whites, blacks, and Mexican Americans in the United States," *American Journal of Clinical*

Nutrition 87:6 (June 2008): 1882–1891. But see Katherine Mangu-Ward, "5 Myths about healthy eating," *Washington Post,* October 16, 2011, B2.

15. K. Giskes et al., "A systematic review of environmental factors and obesogenic dietary intakes among adults: are we getting closer to understanding obesogenic environments?," *Obesity Reviews* 12 (May 2011): e 95-e 106. However, in a 2009 review of food desert research, the US Department of Agriculture, Economic Research Service, Access to Affordable and Nutritious Food: Measuring and Understanding Food Deserts and Their Consequences: Report to Congress, June 2009, v, concluded:

> The causal pathways linking limited access to nutritious food to measures of overweight like Body Mass Index (BMI) and obesity are not well understood. Several studies find that proximity of fast food restaurants and supermarkets are correlated with BMI and obesity. But increased consumption of such healthy foods as fruits and vegetables, low-fat milk, or whole grains does not necessarily lead to lower BMI. Consumers may not substitute away from less healthy foods when they increase their consumption of healthy foods. Easy access to all food, rather than lack of access to specific healthy foods, may be a more important factor in explaining increases in BMI and obesity.

16. Researchers have found: no relationship between greater supermarket unavailability to diet quality and fruit and vegetable consumption (Janne Boone-Heinonen et al., "Fast Food Restaurants and Food Stores," *Archives of Internal Medicine* 171:13 (July 11, 2011): 1162–1170); no connection between the proximity to grocery stores, fast food, and obesity among young children (Helen Lee, "The role of local food availability in explaining obesity risk among young school-aged children," *Social Science & Medicine* 74:8 (April 2012):1193–1203); and no relationship between school and residential food environment and children's diet in California (Ruopeng An and Roland Storm, "School and Residential Neighborhood Food Environment and Diet Among California Youth," *American Journal of Preventive Medicine* 42:2 (February 2012): 129–135). See also Neil Wrigley, Daniel Warm, Barrie Margetts, "Depreviation, diet, and food-retail access: findings from the Leeds 'food deserts' study," *Environment & Planning Annual* 35:1 (January 2003): 151–188; Neil Wrigley et al., "The Leeds 'food deserts' intervention study: what the focus groups reveal," *International Journal of Retail & Distribution Management* 32:2/3 (February 2004): 123–136; Sarah Kliff, "The $900,000 corner store experiment," *Washington Post,* June 10, 2012, G1.

17. Kathryn Colasanti, Charlotte Litjens, Michael Hamm, Growing Food in the City: The Production Potential of Detroit's Vacant Land, C. S. Mott Group for Sustainable Food Systems at Michigan State University, June 2010, 7 (Figure 3: Local Production Capacity) and Kathryn J. A. Colasanti and Michael W. Hamm, "Assessing the local food supply capacity of Detroit, Michigan," *Journal of Agriculture, Food Systems, and Community Development* 1:2 (Fall 2010): 41–58, at 51 (Table 2. Acreage Needed to Supply Current and Recommended Consumption). See generally, Kathryn J. A. Colasanti, Growing Food in the City: Two Approaches to Exploring Scaling-Up Urban Agriculture in Detroit, Master of Science Thesis, Michigan State University

2009 <ProQuest Dissertations and Theses>. But see Richard C. Longworth, "Forget Urban Farms. We Need Walmart," January 7, 2011 <www.good.is/post> (August 5, 2011).

18. Sharanbir S. Grewal and Parwinder S. Grewal, "Can cities become self-reliant in food," *Cities* 29: 1 (February 2012): 1–11, and DWP, Phase One: Research and Priorities: Policy Audit Topic: Environmental Remediation and Health, December 16, 2010, 3.3 (Existing Conditions and Trends: The Role of Soil Conditions in Urban Agriculture). See also John Gallagher, "In Detroit, even a vacant lot is useful," *Detroit Free Press,* September 26, 2010, A32, and Hodgson, Campbell, Bailkey, Urban Agriculture, 21–22, 28–31.

19. Sharanbir S. Grewal et al., "An assessment of soil rematode food webs and nutrient pools in community gardens and vacant lots in two post-industrial American cities," *Urban Ecosystems* 14:2 (June 2011): 181–184.

20. See, e.g., D. Blair, C. C. Giesecke, S. Sherman, "A Dietary Social and Economic Evaluation of the Philadelphia Urban Gardening Project," *Journal of Nutrition Education* 23:4 (July–August 1991): 161–167 (in comparison to nongardeners, gardeners in the study ate six of fourteen vegetable categories significantly more frequently; gardening was positively associated with community involvement and life satisfaction); Autumn K. Hanna and Pikai Oh, "Rethinking Urban Poverty: A Look at Community Gardens," *Bulletin of Science, Technology & Society* 20:3 (June 2000): 207–216; Gary P. Green et al., "Community-Based Economic Development Projects Are Small but Valuable," *Rural Development Perspectives* 9:3(1993): 8–15; Gail Feenstra, Sharyl McGrew, David Campbell, Entrepreneurial Community Gardens: Growing Food, Skills, Jobs and Communities, Publication 21587, University of California, Agriculture and Natural Resources, 1999.

21. Lewis D. Solomon and Melissa B. Kirgis, "Business Cooperatives: A Primer," *DePaul Business Law Journal* 6:2 (Spring/Summer 1994):223–289. See generally Frank T. Adams and Gary B. Hansen, *Putting Democracy to Work: A Practical Guide for Starting and Managing Worker-Owned Businesses,* rev. ed. (San Francisco: Berrett-Kaehler, 1992).

22. See, e.g., Sally McGrane, "An Effort to Bury a Throwaway Culture One Repair at a Time," *New York Times,* May 9, 2012, A10.

23. For a study of the role of Latino gardens in community development, see Laura Saldivar-Tanaka and Marianne E. Krasny, "Culturing community development, neighborhood open space, and civic agriculture: The case of Latino community gardens in New York City," *Agriculture and Human Values* 21 (Winter 2004): 399–412.

24. Lewis D. Solomon and Tricia Asaro, "Community-Based Health Care: A Legal and Policy Analysis," *Fordham Urban Law Journal* 24:2 (Winter 1997) 6: 235–313. See also Suzy Hansen, "Hope in the Wreckage," *New York Times Magazine,* July 29, 2012, 22–29, and David Beito, *From Mutual Aid to the Welfare State: Fraternal Societies and Social Services, 1890–1967* (Chapel Hill, NC: University of North Carolina, 2000).

25. City of Detroit, Planning and Development Department, Application For Garden Permit/Adopt-A-Lot Permit, n.d.

26. Charter of the City of Detroit, January 1, 2012, Section 4-112 and Detroit Planning and Development Department, Development Land Sales Request: Urban Renewal Land/Surplus Property Under Development Agreement: Standard

Procedure for the Purchase of Urban Renewal Land <www.ci.detroit.mi.us/ BusinessDevelopment/DevelopmentLandSalesRequests/tabid/1145/Default. aspx> (July 3, 2012).

In southwest Detroit, the Bing administration offered to sell 300 city-owned lots in that area to the adjacent property owners, pursuant to the Adjacent Vacant Lot Program. The property owner sends in $200 for one lot, together with simple paperwork and receives the deed along with a gift card to purchase a fence for the property. Dave Bing, Mayor, City of Detroit, 2012 State of the City Address, March 7, 2012, 8. See also Cecil Angel, "Neighbors left, now services disappear," *Detroit Free Press*, May 20, 2012, A1, and Laura Berman, "'Progress' fuels city hopes," *Detroit Free Press*, March 13, 2012, A3. The city council extended the program for five years through June 30, 2017 with property owners able to buy two lots.

For the Michigan Land Bank Fast Track Authority Adjacent Lot Disposition Program, see DWP, Neighborhood, Community Development & Housing, 3.4 (Initiatives: Land: Adjacent Lot Disposition Program).

For a discussion of the importance of land tenure arrangements and land disposition policies, see Hodgson, Campbell, Bailkey, Urban Agriculture, 24–27, 51–52.

27. See, e.g., Vicki Been and Ioan Voicu, "The Effect of Community Gardens on Neighboring Property Values," New York University Law and Economic Working Papers, Paper 46, March 2006.

28. John E. Mogk quoted in Kristin Choo, "Plow Over," *ABA Journal* 97 (August 2011): 43–49, 56, 70, at 49.

29. Michigan Compiled Laws Section 286.471.

30. Michigan Department of Agriculture & Rural Development, Generally Accepted Agricultural and Management Practices for Site Selection and Odor Control for New and Expanding Livestock Production Facilities, January 2012, iii, and Michigan Commission of Agriculture & Rural Development, Meeting Minutes, December 14, 2011, 13–14. See also Dawson Bell, "State helps Detroit with urban farming," *Detroit Free Press*, December 15, 2011, A4.

31. Matthew Dolan, "New Detroit Farm Plan Taking Root," *Wall Street Journal*, July 6, 2012, A3. See also John Gallagher, "Big farming projects might be under way by next spring in Detroit," *Detroit Free Press*, October 8, 2012 <LexisNexis>; John Gallagher, "Farm plan close to reality for Detroit," *Detroit Free Press*, July 5, 2012, A1; Laura Berman, "Urban farming idea slowly sprouts," *Detroit News*, March 20, 2012, A3; John Gallagher, "Finally growing," *Detroit Free Press*, November 19, 2011, C1; John Gallagher, "Commercial farm to start in Detroit with 1,000 Trees," *Detroit Free Press*, August 8, 2011, A1; Laura Berman, "Cultivating urban farm becomes lengthy process," *Detroit News*, February 24, 2011, A4; Laura Berman, "Entrepreneur finds Detroit farming a slow go," *Detroit News*, April 6, 2010, A3; David Whitford, "Can Farming Save Detroit?," *Fortune* 161:1 (January 18, 2010): 78–84; John Gallagher, "Farm could make Detroit hot spot for fresh foods," *Detroit Free Press*, April 2, 2009, NWS14.

32. For a helpful model for urban agriculture in residential districts, see City of Cleveland, Zoning Code, Agriculture in Residential Districts Sections 337.02 (One-Family Districts), 337.25 (Agricultural Uses in Residential Districts),

and 347.02 (Restrictions on the Keeping of Farm Animals and Bees). See also, Hodgson, Campbell, Bailkey, Urban Agriculture, 74–79, and Schwarz, "Re-thinking the Places in Between," in *Rebuilding America's Legacy Cities*, 177–178.

The proposed Detroit Urban Agriculture Ordinance recognizes agriculture as a permitted use. It puts no size limits on urban farms and allows the sale of produce through various avenues, from farm stands on the property to farmers' markets and directly to retail and wholesale, public or private entities. The draft prohibits farm animals from being produced on an urban garden or urban farm. City of Detroit, City Planning Commission, Draft, Urban Agriculture Ordinance, September 12, 2012.

For a discussion of zoning for urban agriculture see Hodgson, Campbell, Bailkey, Urban Agriculture, 48–50.

33. See generally, Lewis D. Solomon, *Rethinking Our Centralized Monetary System: The Case for a System of Local Currencies* (Westport, CT: Praeger, 1996).
34. Ibid., 43–51. See also Wikipedia, "Ithaca Hours" <www.en.wikipedidia.org/wiki/Ithaca_Hours> (July 17, 2012), and Paul Glover, "Creating Community Economics with Local Currency" and "Ithaca Hour Factsheet" <www.paulglover.org/hourintro.html> (July 17, 2012).
35. US Constitution, Article I, Section 10, clause 1.
36. 18 USC, Sections 486 and 491.
37. 18 USC, Section 491. See also Solomon, *Rethinking*, 95–127.

9

Conclusion: Evaluating the Likelihood of Success

Since 2009, the first stirrings of revitalization have occurred in Detroit after decades of free fall. Detroit has substantial assets, including numerous anchor institutions, particularly for-profit business and locally and nationally based foundations, on which to build its revival. However, reconstruction faces many negatives, including massive population losses; a shrinking tax base; too few jobs; an uneducated, unskilled workforce; and many impoverished families. A legacy of budgetary shortfalls, municipal corruption, distrust, high crime rates, a lack of quality public services, and inadequate public schools all exist. Intransigent municipal employees' and teachers' unions—focused on members' self-interest—as well as their political allies impede progress. The totality of these liabilities poses significant, but not insurmountable, obstacles to Detroit's revival, especially if various solutions are sought one by one.

Analyzing the probabilities for successful revival with respect to three key areas—public finances, schools, and jobs—falls into three categories: probable (but there are no guarantees); possible; and remote.

The highest probabilities of success may occur in the public sector. Encouraging steps have taken place in meeting public-sector challenges. The 2013 appointment of an emergency manager offers the prospect of Detroit averting insolvency, balancing its budget, and regaining its fiscal stability and sustainability, despite the opposition of public-sector unions and their political allies. The specter of bankruptcy looms over Detroit, if the city cannot bring its falling revenues in line with its expenses. The financial viability of the Detroit Public School District also appears probable, particularly with the enactment of the 2012 Local Financial Stability and Choice Act, but enrollment declines raise budgetary difficulties.

A resurgent for-profit private sector, both established firms and entrepreneurial start-ups, but not the Creative Class, will probably propel economic growth and job creation. The upward trend of economic development will help the city rebuild its tax base and generate some jobs for residents.

Detroit faces, however, massive human capital and labor-market challenges. A mismatch exists between available jobs and adult residents' skills and education levels. It is problematic whether workforce development efforts, even with additional funding, can supply the requisite remediation. An adult workforce composed of many unskilled, uneducated individuals probably will not find employment in the vibrant tech and health care sectors, thereby placing the likelihood of a substantial reduction in Detroit's unemployment rate as only a possibility. A mismatch also exists between where workers live and where jobs are located. The creation of a regional transit authority, designed to coordinate the city and suburban bus systems and build and operate a bus rapid transit system, will help overcome the spatial mismatch.

Enhanced academic performance of Detroit's K–12 public students appears a low possibility, despite the positive steps taken by the two state-appointed managers. Reducing students' huge educational deficit encounters some parental disinterest in their children's education and the opposition of the teachers' union and its political allies.

Concentrating public services in more densely populated neighborhoods and land-use reconfiguration will likely remain aspiration strategies, either one filled with political risks in adoption and maintenance. The 2011 short-term public service delivery action plan, to date, has achieved only modest results. Low odds exist for the implementation of any type of comprehensive, municipal planning effort, at least for the foreseeable future.

In addition to the traditional public and private sectors—the latter including both for-profit businesses and nonprofit foundations—as a remote possibility, Detroiters may build an alternative political economy sector. Despite numerous obstacles, practical, legal, psychological, and cultural, a bottom-up development strategy oriented around grassroots groups could not only empower people but also open opportunities based on using vacant land and unskilled labor. Recognizing that significant levels of local self-reliance, beginning with food, are possible, urban agriculture could serve as a major engine for Detroit's revitalization. Building a community-based food system could enable residents to achieve broader goals, such as increased employment and, ultimately, a more sustainable, more self-sufficient, parallel political economy sector serving basic human needs. Residents would use local resources to meet most of their needs while strengthening neighborhoods.

The development of communities from within rests, however, on residents' determination and involvement, both of which remain very uncertain. Also, embarking on a cultural change is difficult; a change from entitlement to risk-taking, whether for-profit entrepreneurship or cooperative self-sufficiency, is even more difficult, thereby resulting in low odds for the implementation of an alternative political economy sector.

Index